QUALITY CIRCLES IN ACTION

Quality Circles in Action

Mike Robson

Gower

Published by
Gower Publishing Company Limited,
Gower House,
Croft Road,
Aldershot,
Hants GU11 3HR,
England

Gower Publishing Company,
Old Post Road,
Brookfield,
Vermont 05036,
USA
Reprinted 1985,1988

Robson, Mike
   Quality circles in action.
   1. Quality circles – Great Britain –
   Case studies
   I. Title
   658.4   HD66

   ISBN 0-566-02433-0

Typeset in Great Britain by
Graphic Studios (Southern) Ltd., Godalming, Surrey
Printed and bound in Great Britain
by Billings & Sons Limited, Worcester.

Contents

Preface

Five years ago the Quality Circles approach was dismissed by many in the UK as just another gimmick. Today it is clear that, when introduced with skill and care, Quality Circles can be an important and permanent part of an organisation's management style, and they are used in an estimated 500–750 organisations. The newly-formed National Society for Quality Circles already has over 100 members, representing over 2,500 Quality Circles, and the number is growing fast.

Against this background, it is rather surprising that so little serious case material has been published and it is this lack that has prompted the present volume. It brings together a range of case histories from eight companies representing a wide spread of manufacturing and non-manufacturing industry. They deal with the introduction and maintenance of Quality Circles, and also with many of the difficulties which can occur. Having been involved with the introduction of QC programmes in a large number of companies, both in the UK and in Europe, I am constantly aware of both the similarities and the differences among organisations and their methods of introduction. One thing, however, is clear, and that is that if the concept is introduced as a part of a long-term managerial philosophy, and if great care is taken to abide by the principles which underlie the approach, then it will work and will continue working; if not, it will be difficult to sustain.

The organisations which contributed to the book were assisted by different consultant firms and were given varying levels of help. Since the prime purpose of the book is to explore Quality Circles in action, the names of the different consultancies used have been deliberately obscured. On the other hand any comments or observations about consultants in general and the need for them in helping to introduce Quality Circles have been left in.

Complete freedom was given to the authors of the case histories to tackle the subject as they saw fit and this is reflected in the variety of their presentations. I have prefaced each contributed chapter with an introductory section, set in small type, designed to highlight the key points.

In addition to the case histories the book also contains several other sections. In talking to many hundreds of people about Quality Circles I am often astounded by the number and range of misconceptions held. Quality Circles is actually a precise mechanism and should not be confused with other vehicles for solving problems and making the most of opportunities. I have therefore included a chapter which reviews and re-states the elements of Quality Circles. Secondly, many people are concerned about what happens to Quality Circles when the first flush of enthusiasm has died away. There are some important lessons to be learned here and they are addressed in Part II. Also in Part II is a chapter on the main causes of failure in a Quality Circles programme. This is particularly necessary since the case histories in the book all feature programmes that have been more or less successful. I was unable to persuade any organisation that had completely failed with the approach to contribute a case history.

Obviously it is desirable for organisations running QC programmes to learn by studying the experience of others. For those about to install a programme – or perhaps merely contemplating the possibility – access to 'real life' examples is especially valuable. My hope is that the present book will provide guidance and stimulus in all such cases.

My thanks are due to all those who wrote the case histories and to all the QC members who made the articles possible.

Mike Robson

Quality Circles – a reminder

The Quality Circles concept is universal, with literally millions of people involved, covering all continents of the world. Though Quality Circles first developed in Japan during the late 1950s and early 1960s, the approach is based on Western theories of management, notably Douglas McGregor's 'Theory Y'. At the outset it is important to understand how Quality Circles should be viewed and what place the concept should have in an organisation, for if it is treated merely as another management technique it is unlikely to stand the test of time.

Simply, if introduced properly Quality Circles represents part of a coherent managerial philosophy. It is not a 'stand alone' concept, but forms one aspect of 'the way we want to do things around here'; there is little point in introducing Quality Circles into a company where the rest of the management style is incompatible and compatible activities are not the norm in the rest of the organisation. Indeed the most common cause of failure with Quality Circles is their introduction into businesses which have not really thought through the implications in terms of their management·philosophy. This aspect is covered in more depth in Part II.

The essentials of Quality Circles

So what is this concept all about? In a sentence, Quality Circles is an approach which allows employees to become more involved by solving their own job-related problems in an organised way. It sounds simple, but in fact this is deceptive, and if we analyse the definition we can isolate a number of reasons for this.

Firstly, Quality Circles is an approach which allows people to become more involved, but puts no pressure on them to do so; in other words the approach is entirely voluntary at all levels of the organisation. If a manager objects to the concept there will be no Quality Circles in his department unless or until he changes his mind. Even if he does decide to support the concept, if his supervisors do not volunteer, no groups will be formed, and similarly if the supervisor is willing but no volunteers are forthcoming from the workforce. This principle of voluntariness is crucial to the success of Quality Circles, so much so that we can state categorically that if it is not voluntary then it is not Quality Circles. It is, however, not an easy thing to introduce and to manage, since it is such an unusual notion. In the working life of the average employee one rather suspects that nothing is really voluntary, and it takes more than a mere statement to make the principle of voluntariness a reality. Recently, when a group of supervisors were having the Quality Circle concept explained to them as a part of its introduction to their company, one of them asked for reassurance that it really was voluntary. Having received confirmation, he proceeded to say, 'OK, I understand. Now, in our organisation we have an appraisal scheme and it so happens that in three weeks' time my boss has to write his annual report about me. Can you absolutely guarantee me that if I don't join in it will have no effect on my appraisal?' There is of course no guarantee, and even if one was offered there might still be doubts, and therefore pressures, if it were not fully credible. Because it's an unusual principle, voluntariness needs to be managed with great care.

The second distinctive feature of the Quality Circles approach is that the people who join in are encouraged to solve their own job-related problems. When asked to state what problems affect them at work, most people tend to point to difficulties caused by other sections, departments, or people rather than to factors that lie within their own sphere of influence. This inevitably causes frustration and tends to be a circular process, since for every finger pointed there is usually at least one pointing back. Quality Circles overcome this major difficulty of participative problem solving by introducing the combined ideas of 'No finger pointing' and 'Put your own house in order'. By focusing on issues that they can themselves influence, Quality Circles are in a much stronger position to get things done than if they spend their time trying to tell others what to do.

The third feature of the Quality Circles definition is that the members solve their problems in an organised way; in other words they are given training in the skills of systematic problem solving and of working together effectively in a group. Quality Circles is probably the only approach which gives such training to non-supervisory staff. Training is an important part of the concept since it gives members the tools to do the job. It should be remembered that for most staff and many supervisors as well this will be the first time that they will have been involved in such an activity, and it would be very dangerous to assume that the requisite skills were necessarily already in place and ready to be used. Indeed it is difficult to see how a Quality Circles programme could really succeed without training being an integral part of it.

So it can be seen that the approach is not nearly as simple as it appears. It needs to form a part of the philosophy of management of the organisation and it must be voluntary, with the emphasis on 'putting our own house in order'. Furthermore, training must be given to enable groups to engage in the problem-solving activity in an organised and professional way.

The mechanism

So much for the concept. In rather more detail, a Quality Circle consists of a group of four to ten volunteers who work for the same first-line supervisor and who meet together regularly to identify, analyse and solve their work problems. A number of points are worth highlighting here.

Firstly, Quality Circles is a natural workgroup approach as distinct from a task-force or project-group process. Project groups are task-specific and therefore their effective lifespan tends to be related to the problem they are solving. Furthermore, since they bring together people who would not otherwise have been together and because the task is handed to them, such groups are invariably 'owned' by the management. This is not, of course, to say that they are ineffective or inferior, merely that they are different from Quality Circles.

The second point to highlight is that the group does not need to consist of the entire workforce from that section. If twenty people work in an area and nine of them volunteer, then the nine form the Quality Circle. Of course, the remaining eleven must be kept informed at all times about the topics being tackled and should be encouraged to put forward their ideas even if they do not want to join the group.

Thirdly, the groups meet regularly once a week, for an hour, and in paid time. Once a week is a good practical balance between the desire to get on with things on the one hand, and the need to ensure that the workflow in the section is not adversely affected on the other. The meetings should be limited in length as an antidote to Parkinson's Law, and experience shows that an hour is the right length of time in most circumstances. Finally on this subject, the meetings should be held in paid time. This is because they are work, not leisure, and as such should be paid in the normal way; no more, no less. Incidentally, do not believe that all Japanese Quality Circles operate in people's own time; that is not so, and the vast majority meet during the normal working day.

Fourthly, the groups, at their meetings, do not stop at the identification of problems for passing on to management for solution; they utilise the training they receive to analyse and solve them, and then to present their own findings to management. A number of vital parts of this process are worth reinforcing. It is the group that selects the issue to be studied; it is not up to management to assign problems to be tackled, although if it wishes the group can ask for advice. In investigating the problem, the group collects data about it so that the solution will be based on facts rather than opinions. This is essential, since it means that the group will be talking the same language as management when they present their findings. The decisions about implementation are taken by the relevant level of management. If the solution is accepted, the Quality Circle monitors and evaluates results to ensure that the predicted outcomes are achieved. Quality Circles, then, are fullscale problem-solving groups, and this factor accounts for much of the satisfaction that the groups derive from the approach.

The aims
Turning to the objectives of a Quality Circles programme, there are three main possible goals: staff involvement, people development and the generation of tangible benefits. As far as staff involvement is concerned it is possible to isolate two broad categories: indirect methods, which are usually based on representative councils, committees and, of course, trade unions; and more direct approaches which ultimately enable all members of staff to play their part in an active way. Both methods are necessary in most organisations, their objectives being both different and compatible, and Quality Circles must not be seen as a threat to the first category. For encouraging direct involvement across a broad front the Quality Circles concept is unquestionably the best mechanism.

The second objective is the development of people in the organisation. Quality Circles undoubtedly promotes the development of staff, through acquisition of new skills and the opportunity to work together on 'real world' problems, and they also help supervisors to build their problem-solving skills and their abilities in working in and leading small groups. Furthermore, for many managers Quality Cirlces offers the practical framework for introducing and developing genuinely participative management styles. Often, in the past, well-meaning attempts by managers to do this have foundered for want of a usable, practical framework, and after a few months 'participation' has been relegated to the back burner with the comment that it 'sounds all right in theory, but . . . '. Quality Circles change this. Although based on sound theoretical premises, the approach is intensely practical, and it builds the bridge back from the training room to the real world.

The third goal of Quality Circles is to generate benefits for the organisation and the people in it. The evidence suggests that Quality Circles programmes tend to be cost-effective and sometimes dramatically so. Paybacks of fifteen times the investment have been reported occasionally. A vital concern about this, however, is that it is very dangerous to make this objective the primary one, since doing so will involve endangering, maybe breaking, some of the rules, notably that the groups decide which problem to tackle and that there is no pressure on them to select one which has any direct tangible benefits. If this happens, the ownership of the group has been 'stolen' and the concept becomes just another management-controlled and regulated technique.

So it is important to recognise that the goals of a Quality Circles programme should be, firstly to provide a genuine means for staff to become more involved, and secondly to give people throughout the organisation the opportunity of developing their skills. The third goal in

order of importance is the generation of tangible benefits. This is very much the third priority and indeed some
companies, such as ITT, do not measure these at all
unless the individual Circles want to.

Quality Circles is an exciting, invigorating and fresh
concept. If introduced with care and skill there is no
doubt that it can contribute to the development of
healthier and more effective organisations where
people's abilities at all levels are recognised and valued
and there is an opportunity provided for latent talent to
be used.

Part I

QUALITY CIRCLES AT WORK

Preparing the ground
I: British Telecom

Ken Burfitt

The British Telecom case history is interesting in a number of quite unconnected respects. Firstly, it is the only properly organised programme that I am aware of where the facilitator is the 'in-line' middle manager, two levels senior to the Quality Circle leaders. It should be stated that this arrangement was introduced for practical and necessary reasons in this case and worked well. It does not necessarily indicate any policy on the part of British Telecom that this is either the only, or the correct arrangement for resourcing the programme. It may be worthwhile, however, examining the arrangement since, in unskilled hands, it could present two potential problems: one, the effect on the manager between the Circle and the facilitator, and two, the effect on the Quality Circle group itself. As far as the manager in the middle is concerned, the big danger is that he feels left out and thereby threatened by the whole process. In this instance considerable efforts were made to ensure that any feelings of anxiety were quickly dispelled and that those concerned were kept fully in the picture, but this does not necessarily completely solve the problem. The extent of the difficulty is likely to be significantly affected by the confidence of the person in the middle and also the relationship between him and both his subordinates and his boss. The second potential danger in having an in-line facilitator is the reaction of the Quality Circle members themselves. Many experts on small group working within organisations claim that it is dangerous to have three or more levels of a hierarchy together in one task group, since this often brings with it hidden agendas, defensiveness and apprehension. The facilitator role in Quality Circles is rather different, since it is not really a

11

member role, but there are similar dangers. The 'classical' Quality Circle model calls for facilitators who are not in the direct line above the group, and it does this with good reason in most cases.

The second noteworthy aspect of the British Telecom case concerns the role of the trade unions, and the handling of a difficult union situation. The case makes very clear that the unions were consulted at all stages, which is a prerequisite of any form of success. However, the history also reveals that the unions did not actively support the programme, but rather allowed it to proceed as a field trial without any real enthusiasm. It is easy to lapse into unproductive win/lose attitudes in this situation, and most important that this is not allowed to happen. Quality Circles is a part of a very different way of doing things than has usually been the case in the past, and it would be unrealistic to expect everyone to welcome it enthusiastically from the outset. A genuinely committed management would continue to press not only for consent but for active collaboration and involvement. Fortunately there is an increasing number of trade union representatives who are willing actively to support programmes in their companies, and also to talk to more sceptical colleagues in other organisations about the merits of the approach when introduced with the right motives in the right way. In some environments it will take a long time to repair the damage done by traditional 'us and them' attitudes and to replace them with more constructive ones based on developing higher levels of mutual respect and trust. There are no simple ways of achieving this: it takes long-term commitment, the ability to communicate clearly, determination, courage and imagination, and even then there is no cast-iron guarantee of success.

If a trade union remains worried about aspects of the Quality Circles approach, it will sometimes help to set up a steering committee, thus involving the union in the management and control of the programme. A further safeguard is to begin with a pilot scheme which can be mounted and evaluated, with union involvement, before any widespread introduction is decided upon. Visits to other organisations can also help, especially when freedom is given to have private discussions with their opposite numbers. It is worth reinforcing at this point that the approach calls for high levels of individual respect and trust, that the environment must be provided within which these can develop and flourish, and furthermore that it is usually the task of management to make the first moves in creating this opportunity.

The final point to note about the British Telecom case history is the care with which they evaluated the concept and prepared the ground before deciding on an introduction. For most organisations, Quality Circles represents a significant step in terms of philosophy and management style and deserves much careful thought before a decision is made. This may seem an obvious observation, but too many companies have introduced Quality Circles as the latest 'flavour of the month'. They have paid the price for this and, maybe worse, may have tarnished the good name and reputation of genuine Quality Circles programmes.

Graeme Whitecross, British Telecom Cardiff General Manager, was questioning a Quality Circle after their presentation of solutions to management. 'What are your feelings about taking part in Quality Circles?' he had asked, and the discussion had extended for some time. Then one of the Circle members, knowing that Quality Circles were still on trial, and gaining confidence from the General Manager's evident interest, said, 'You have asked us about *our* thoughts, now what are *you* going to do about Circles?' 'I need to see presentations from all Circles before I decide,' the General Manager replied, 'I am very impressed with what I have seen here.' At which another Circle member interposed, 'Whatever you decide to do, we are going to carry on anyway.' That statement speaks volumes for the effect Circles can have on the participants, and I am tempted to stop there and say QED. But that would not do justice to the concept, which has less to do with the actual outcome and more to do with the way of achieving it.

What, then, was the attraction of Quality Circles to British Telecom, Cardiff? Traditionally, problems are management's job to deal with! If management are too busy, too thick, or just couldn't care less, why should we bother about it? Does that have a familiar ring? It does to me. In fact, it's a little too close to home for comfort. Now, I believe that British Telecom staff are as good as any anywhere. Indeed, the fact that they have worked so well, for so long, within a rigid hierarchical structure involving separated Sales, Installation, Maintenance, Works, Planning, Customer Service, Finance and Personnel functions, sometimes with different objectives, will testify to that. Procedural documents covered every possible eventuality, so how could problems exist? Because somewhere, somehow, people were in danger of being forgotten. *People* who are customers, *people* who are staff, *people* who are managers, all exerted their different pressures on the British Telecom system which only *people* can relieve. There were problems; indeed, some staff had so succumbed to the system that they accepted poor stores supply as the norm and represented it as the required standard.

Preparing the ground

I would like to claim that British Telecom, Cardiff, quickly recognised the virtues of problem solving within Quality Circles, but that would not be correct. Much of the available literature on Quality Circles and associated case histories did not mirror British Telecom operations, and so, with union agreement, consultants were invited in for a day in November 1981 to examine the Sales and Installation control function as possible areas for introducing the concept. Their belief was that the control function, with sales staff reporting up the line to engineers, reinforced by separate union representation, did not lend itself easily to Quality Circles. However, they felt that the engineering installation field force, which fitted telephones and switching apparatus in customers' premises, was a fertile area to explore.

This encouragement might have led them to go ahead with Circles there and then, but slowly a realisation was emerging. It was that word again – people. People make

Circles work. Circles cannot make people work. If people do not want Circles they will fail them. We needed to find out if the British Telecom system needed Circles and, equally, if staff wished to participate. Accordingly the consultants were commissioned to do a two-week study, with union agreement, visiting and accompanying staff about their daily tasks. The resulting report in May 1982 was interesting in that it found the staff 'good, confident, independently capable, analytical and receptive to Circles'. If they were all of these things why were they interested in belonging to Circles? British Telecom already provided briefing sessions, communication sessions, team talks, suggestion schemes; and union history in joint production participation was good! The reason people were interested was that none of these schemes involve organised problem solving and Quality Circles promised to get things done at last.

The ball was now firmly in the Cardiff Area Board's court. Should they proceed, and if so, how? The least expensive course was to buy a package of material and commence it ourselves. The most expensive course was to engage consultants' help for its introduction, but this was the option chosen. With the knowledge I now have of Circles I know the decision was the right one. The hands-on assistance that develops Circles is best given by those who already have the experience of what to do and when to do it.

The next step clearly was to introduce Quality Circles to all staff concerned, but how best to do it? The consultant team favoured a careful, step-by-step approach, so this is what we adopted. British Telecom unions traditionally speak for the staff, and their support or, at the very least, lack of objection was a prime requirement. Accordingly an introductory presentation to the representatives of the three union branches involved was held in July 1982. Two of the branches represented the engineering technical grades – the prospective members of Circles, and one branch the supervisors involved – the facilitators and leaders. At this meeting, two branches were unenthusiastic about the concept, believing that the existing system, if used properly, provided many ways in which problems were notified to management. In their view management too often acted too late and sometimes not at all. They also questioned why leaders should be the natural supervisors. After much discussion, however, they agreed that Circles could go ahead provided genuine discussions on other outstanding issues took place. The managers' union branch were happy as long as they had the facility to monitor progress. Quality Circles was made the subject of an official Field Trial so that it could be properly evaluated.

Now it would be easy to register this as a success, but not in my view. Oh yes, we had the OK to proceed, but we had, at our first real test, failed to enlist the active support of union people. The unions had seen some threats in Circles, and the concept demands the removal of threats. The care with which we had put the presentation together was not enough. We would have to convince people that Quality Circles was worthy of their participation.

Getting started
The eligible staff at the depots concerned are under the first-line supervision of inspectors. After an introductory presentation, all eight inspectors volunteered for the leader training course and in the event seven attended, one being on leave. The course, of three days' duration, was run by the consultant and included the facilitators. The early part of it dealt with the group process, gradually developing by the use of key tapes into practical problem solving, and culminating on the last day with a presentation of solutions to invited British Telecom managers. The course was considered by those attending to be highly successful, but the most interesting feature was the change in the participants themselves. They may

have come on the course for differing reasons – some interested, some curious, some not to be seen to refuse – but during the three days the Circle concept had so added to relationships that their improved confidence in expressing themselves and their beliefs was clear to everyone. This, then, was a success: people trying something and feeling good about it. No wonder at the end of the course all seven volunteered to be leaders.

Now, as I have explained earlier, the prospective members of Circles were telephone apparatus fitters, and line and telephone installers. They report to their depots at the start of the day and return at finishing time. Only occasionally would they return during the day, and then for a special reason. The best time for Circles to meet would be either the first hour or the last hour. Why, you may ask? Well, the obvious reason – and the wrong one – is that management felt that it would cost the business less to have meetings when the staff are normally on site. But let us look deeper into Circles. We are inviting people to take part on a voluntary basis; to feel free, in their ownership of Circles, to take consensus views of problems, and to seek win/win solutions. They themselves would not wish to meet at a time which clearly instituted a new problem and imposed a cost penalty. The difference is perhaps a subtle one, but nonetheless significant.

Seven Circles meeting once a week during the first hour of the day would monopolise depot meeting rooms and require more than one facilitator. With these constraints, it was decided to begin with four. This was fully explained to the inspectors and willingly they agreed amongst themselves the four groups to start with, the other three waiting until later. Introductory presentations were then made to each of the four workgroups, at the end of which they were asked to signify within three days if they wished to become a member of a Circle. In the event all four groups started Circles, with between eight and twelve members each. Interestingly, after five

months, with two Circles having completed presentations of solutions to management, and two Circles ready
to present, only four people had left the Circles, all of
whom gave reasons unconnected with the operation.

Essential to the whole programme has been the
voluntary aspect. Volunteering can, of course, be for a
variety of reasons. Some may have volunteered for
selfish reasons – to impress the supervisor; some
because it sounded better than working; some because
they were genuinely interested in the concept; and some
because they were curious. Does it really matter? In fact,
I believe that the most crucial factor in people joining
Circles is not the volunteering in, but everyone knowing
that they can volunteer out whenever they desire! Once
in, it is the skill of the facilitator and leader in helping
members to enjoy the experience which will sustain the
success. Some reader will surely say that that is an
interpersonal skill, and he would probably be right. It is
important to ensure that everyone talks and listens to
each other, and that the communication is genuinely
two-way.

The facilitator

British Telecom employs its own training staff, and the
Quality Circle programme could have been considered
in Cardiff as a training concern. Indeed, some of the
Circle problem-solving techniques would have been
familiar to training staff. I believe, however, that the
Cardiff decision to encourage the in-line middle manager
to be facilitator has much to recommend it:

– the careful building of beliefs in the Circle process is as
  important to the facilitator as to the Circle members;
– much of the practical operation of the Circle lies within
  the direct authority and responsibility of the in-line
  middle manager;
– he is familiar with the technicalities and practices
  under discussion during problem solving;

– relationships so developed are equally useful to the Circle member and to the middle manager.

Of course, ideally the facilitator should be detached for the time necessary to institute Circles – in the Cardiff case about two and a half days per week, with the facilitator attending all four Circle meetings and being fully involved in the preparation and review of the meetings. This is important during the training period. By adding the facilitator role to an existing full middle-manager load we put pressure on both functions; in retrospect, this was a mistake.

The meeting place

As I said earlier, it was the availability of suitable meeting rooms that determined the number of initial Circles. Those at the subsidiary depots ran quite smoothly. The two at the main depot, however, ran into early problems that illustrate some dangers. Some six weeks into the programme long-awaited structural alterations to the meeting room area were started and an alternative room in an adjacent unoccupied building was temporarily allocated.

Temporarily – you know what that means! In this case it meant inadequate lighting and heating in a very large room with glass along two sides, one of which over-looked a main road. And it was winter! Despite our efforts to improve the lighting and arrange portable heating, that room was just as inhospitable when the new room became available as it had been at the beginning. Both Circles had threatened to suspend their operations because of this, and their natural tendency was to reflect on the level of management commitment that would allow this situation to occur. It says something for the Circle process and the enthusiasm of the groups that they did not carry out their threat, and I counted that the first tangible Circle success.

Circle results

Cardiff Quality Circles started meeting in October 1982. Circle A, a group of technicians without vehicles who installed telephone apparatus in customer premises in the town centre, decided to work on the complex issue of improving stores delivery to site. This was normally effected by a stores vehicle co-ordinated to suitable dates and times. If this supply was not complete, the technician often had to return to his local depot to obtain the necessary small items from the subsidiary stores unit. The Circle found that there was no one major problem, but many inter-related operations that could be improved. On collecting data, they identified forty return visits to the stores in four weeks, involving thirty-six hours of time, most for avoidable reasons. They reasoned that the cost to the company – £2,667 over a year – could be considerably reduced, as 65 per cent of the return visits were for readily available small items. Their solutions included rearranging the space in the subsidiary stores so as to provide 80 per cent more capacity in the same area; increasing the holdings of certain small items; and free aspirin for the storeman – also a member of the Circle!

The stores driver, very willing to help even though he was not a Circle member, suggested that he should hold a small stock of the most needed items on his vehicle and be able to replenish it. Dedicated reliefs for both storeman and stores driver were proposed, and the key procedure of initial ordering of stores was improved. Pre-packing small stores and issuing them as a kit is under active consideration, together with the use of a radio-pager.

Circle B was composed of people who installed telephone apparatus in the city outer ring and had their own vehicles. Their choice of objective was to improve daily communications with their central control office, thereby speeding the flow of work and removing frustrations. Whilst they were collecting data about time delays, however, the problems disappeared. Even after some weeks of monitoring, both communication and relationships remained excellent. Our consultant informed us that this is not uncommon with Circles. They are sometimes able to frighten problems away. Checks may show that they are at their most potent when data are being collected, but in some cases even the mere mention of Quality Circles has been sufficient for the problem to vanish. Of course, problems do not die – they lurk, and the Circle system of monitoring a situation where it has acted is often good insurance that the problem will not reappear.

At first this group was rather despondent at having 'lost' its problem, again a common reaction amongst Quality Circles, but then they decided to concentrate on improving their working operations in open plan factory units where long ladders had to be obtained and which involved using three men instead of one for reasons of safety. Their solution, based on data collected, is an easily transported and erected platform which, in their view, will reduce labour costs by one third, and better fulfil safety standards.

Circle C, again mobile fitting technicians, wished to apply themselves to the problems which tended to occur during the first hour of their mornings. During this time, and not usually for the full hour, they had paperwork to complete; they had to telephone their control; they needed to exchange information with each other and their supervisor – and most of this whilst standing at stalls with an inclined writing surface. There were not enough telephones and those that were available were sited away from the stalls. There was ample room for tables and chairs, which increased the frustration, and, indeed, the room was un-affectionately dubbed 'the cattle market'. They argued that none of the morning functions could really be improved whilst such conditions existed, and prepared a revised layout involving enough tables and chairs, and telephones within reach of appropriate groups so that they could be passed from hand to hand, and arranged designated workgroups together so that supervisory functions were made easier. The most interesting development was that, as the Circle progressed, the realisation grew amongst Circle members and managers that the first hour can be crucial to the job satisfaction of the day. The desire to improvise, normal initiatives, correct customer attitudes, and high-standard work are all prejudiced if the first hour is full of frustration. The cost of the furniture was calculated at approximately £250, whilst the Circle claimed that staff would actually leave the depot five minutes earlier because of the better organisation – yearly labour savings of £1,225. These are the savings proposed by the Circle. It will be interesting to see how much of their belief can be accomplished in practice.

Circle D comprised outstation staff who installed the less complex type of telephone apparatus. Because of their remote situation they chose to work initially on the security of their vehicles, which had been the subject of many overnight attacks when parked at the outstation depot. This resulted in losses of batteries, tools and stores, not to mention the cost of the damage and the time lost. Their initial solution, to have their vehicles fitted with hasps and locks, was not effective due to the weakness of the rivets, and this led them to propose a stronger bolted fixing.

They devised a new way of parking their vehicles against the building so that each protected the other. Only the two at the ends were held to be at risk. Adding floodlights to the parking area was also a deterrent.

At the same time the Circle worked on improving the system used to collect special types of telephone from the central stores. Each man made too many individual journeys to the stores, where he had to complete paperwork after, as often as not, standing in a queue. The Circle asked the officers who distributed the work to attend and advise them, which led to better understanding of the problem and even better anticipation of difficulties by the distribution officer. The Circle organised their journeys to collect multiple orders where possible and claimed that this had halved the number of visits necessary.

Preparation for Quality Circles

It will not have escaped your notice that I have dwelt more on the preparation for the introduction of Quality Circles than on the Circle operations. Quite deliberate, I assure you. The first task must be to present the concept honestly to unions, staff and managers, and to re-present where necessary to give the fullest exposure. The nettle to be grasped is to recognise the concept as worthwhile and to prepare carefully. Some may say that the time is not ripe, but will it ever be? This is not a procedure. It is people talking and improving their daily worklives. In British Telecom, for instance, we are currently going through what may turn out to be the most momentous change in our history. The liberalisation of our previous telecommunications monopoly has put pressure on many of the procedures which were previously suitable, and staff are aware that economies are inevitable. Not the time to offer Quality Circles?

During our discussion with the unions, BBC2 ran a television programme showing consultants in the USA and in Britain advising the management of some firms who wished to weaken union power. Not the right time to offer Circles?

In the Cardiff operation some managers even thought that Quality Circles posed a threat to an organisation development programme involving managers, no less. Not the right time to offer Circles? I like to think that all of those reasons are why Quality Circles are needed.

What happens within Quality Circles

Even when started, each Circle had to be nurtured during the training period. There was a natural impatience among members to get on and crack a problem, and this was an evident danger. The message in Circles is that problems are not solved because 'we' are right and 'they' are wrong. Problems are solved because we are all prepared to work at a solution. Every day of our lives we are involved in some win/lose situation and we react more or less from the characteristics formed of many years' experience. It is not possible to change that habit overnight when problem solving. Circle members must be encouraged and allowed the time to evaluate win/win and consensus, and actually feel it to be a better way.

What of the relationships within Circles? Members claim better understanding of each other and of the leader, without prejudice to his role as inspector. Leaders claim a better understanding of staff problems. All welcome the closer relationship with the middle manager facilitator. This again took time to develop. Members admit to some nervousness at the presence of the middle manager in the early stages, but this is largely overcome by encouraging the Circle to own itself. It is important also that the members realise that during Circle meetings they own the leader and facilitator, and the greatest attribute required of the facilitator during the early stages is restraint. I well remember a Circle leader calling it a milestone when a Circle member addressed me by my Christian name. It was; a milestone of confidence.

This developing association with the middle manager does, however, pose its own problem. It leap-frogs the first-line manager above the supervisor, who can therefore feel left out and not committed to supporting the Circle. In Cardiff we needed to recognise this, to reinforce the position of the in-line manager and to work on ensuring his desire to help his Circle staff to reach satisfactory conclusions. As a result he was always part of the management group at presentations of solutions, at the end of the leader course, and at the end of Circle cycles. Together with facilitators he attended progress meetings with the leaders. We supplied him with his own copy of the weekly Circle progress report which went on display in staff rooms and work areas, and all Circles invited him to attend some of their meetings. It is heartening that his comments have been complimentary, especially in respect of the improvement in presentation and people skills now evident in leaders and members.

Summary

I have been asked many times by managers 'What are we getting out of Quality Circles?' 'Can you quantify any improvement in money terms?' 'Can you measure the improvements?' Is this what Circles are about? Not in my view. They are certainly not a panacea. One management decision can overnight negate improvements sought by Circles over months. So why Circles anyway? What is special about the concept? The answer that makes sense to me is this.

Problems we encounter in our daily work operations are composed of:

– things we can solve ourselves – perhaps 20 per cent;
– things we can only solve with others' assistance – say 60 per cent;
– things we can have only a small influence upon – 20 per cent.

The percentage figures are, of course, mine but, whether you wish to adjust them or not, most would agree that the greatest number of problems lie in the middle band. What is really needed to make progress is collective problem solving; consensus amongst those who can affect the cause of the problem; and joint understanding of everyone's point of view. Surely we all need to hold these things dear, and that is the exceptional value that Quality Circles has to offer British Telecom.

Management support has been an essential part of the process in Cardiff. From the very beginning we decided that it had to be shoulder to shoulder and not paternal. This was not easy. I do not know whether you have ever realised it, but many managers love 'get-outs'. They do not go out on limbs unless the saws have all been blunted. Even good managers (like you and me!) are tempted by the lure of the 'get-out'. It actually encourages decisions and discourages commitment, often a recipe for failure. Even Quality Circles has that attraction. If people do not want them, they will not volunteer. After Circles have started, if people do not like them, they will stop them. It is a short step for a manager to rehearse, 'We offered you Quality Circles, you did not want them, now do not moan about problems again.' And, brother, we are back in the old routine – for Quality Circle substitute vicious circle. The message is simple: only take on Circles if you want them to work and are really prepared to work at helping them.

In this case history I have tried to avoid the use of the jargon so loved by consultants, who pigeon-hole every response into a preconceived model. That is fine for robotics, but Quality Circles is about people – people who say silly things, and then follow with sensible things; people who say emotional things and then logical things. It is about people who had words with their wives or husbands that morning or who had too much to drink the previous night. It is about understanding between people who really do know, and it is that knowledge which is often denied to higher managers because they have not sought to answer the needs of their people. How revealing, then, is the comment of a British Telecom Circle member during his Circle's presentation of solutions to higher management.

'We see this as the beginning, not the end.'

Preparing the ground
II: Bally Shoes

Bob Marston and Lesley Rudd

The Bally Shoe Company case history usefully highlights three issues, two of which are of universal interest to organisations thinking about a QC programme or actively involved in one already. The first point, however, is of concern only to companies who use a piecework payment structure. One of the common questions asked by organisations is how well concepts such as Quality Circles can work in highly individualised situations such as those which exist in most shoe manufacturing organisations. The main production departments at Bally are organised as individual work stations with little opportunity for interaction between operatives, and this is reinforced by the nature of the wage structure. Organisations such as Bally should ask themselves whether an approach based on group working can be successful in such an environment, or whether it could be counter-productive? It is possible that an organisation in such a situation would choose to keep individuals apart as much as possible and therefore not to 'risk' the development of a group ethos by introducing Quality Circles or similar concepts. The lesson from Bally, however, is clear: given a commitment to open and participative management, wage structure is not a problem. On a practical note, Circle members are paid at their individual average performance rate for the hour they spend at their meetings.

The second issue of interest concerns the role of facilitator. The case history makes it clear that the programme was in serious danger of collapsing when it was without a facilitator for a couple of months. Research into Quality Circles conducted in America indicates that a primary reason for the failure of Quality Circles programmes is the lack of a facilitator, or insufficient skills amongst those fulfilling the role. In some ways Quality Circles invites employees to change the habits of a lifetime in joining their groups. For most members it will be their first exposure to such a way of working, and there is no doubt that most groups do require assistance, back-up and support, especially in the early months. This is certainly borne out in the Bally case. Without the enthusiasm, commitment, support and gentle prodding offered by the facilitator, groups in their early stages will often begin to lose the discipline of the approach, to miss meetings, and to forget the problem-solving structure. In the Bally case, the problem was caused by an unexpected management reorganisation and, although their programme survived, it was not a happy experience. Since the facilitator's contribution is so crucial, it is not enough merely to have someone who is willing to undertake the role. A considerable amount of training and development is required by most people if they are to be successful in the job.

The third point which is brought out in the case history concerns the leadership of Quality Circles. At Bally there are a number of groups led by people who were previously members of Quality Circles. A question often asked is why the supervisor has to be the leader of the group. The reason is clear: Quality Circles is an approach which works through the normal line structure; it does not set up an alternative organisation which would only serve to confuse and frustrate. It is equally the case that if the supervisor is not committed to the approach it will not work, since he would be more likely to react negatively to ideas proposed by the group. So it is always sensible at least to begin with the supervisor as leader. If in the future for any reason he wishes to withdraw, but to maintain his support, it is then possible to train a member as leader. Indeed, many would argue that this is something to be actively encouraged.

Bally is a brand-conscious manufacturer of high-grade, ladies' fashion footwear, although recently the Company has diversified into the manufacture of men's shoes.

The company is a Swiss-based multinational with manufacturing units in Switzerland, France and the UK. Bally International in turn is part of the large Oerlikon

Buhrle Group. There has been initial interest in Quality Circles in all three manufacturing countries, but it was decided to proceed cautiously, with Bally (UK) being responsible for the pilot studies and scheme.

The manufacturing division of the company, where Quality Circles were first introduced in 1982, employs 850 people in three factories in East Anglia. The payment system for the 600 production employees is predominantly individual payment by results (piecework), and their interests are represented by the National Union of Footwear, Leather and Allied Trades (NUFLAT), a small independent trade union. The administrative employees and management staff are represented by ASTMS (The Association of Scientific, Technical, Managerial and Supervisory Staffs).

Bally encourages open communication in management in motivating its work force. The company operates regular briefing groups, joint consultation committee meetings, twice-yearly staff information events and other usual communication channels such as health and safety committee meetings.

The feasibility stage

An initial interest in Quality Circles developed simultaneously at different levels of management. Three middle managers, having read articles on the concept in late 1981, were sufficiently interested to propose further investigation. At the same time, and coincidentally, two directors attended a presentation given by a firm of consultants and were interested enough to learn more.

The three middle managers, David Leamon and John Anderson (Factory Managers) and Bob Marston (Personnel Manager), were charged with conducting a feasibility study which commenced in May 1981.

The consultants were asked by Bally senior managers to furnish a list of companies who would support their claims of successful Quality Circle introductions. The project team, however, decided to ignore this list and

29

build up their own file of unsolicited testimonials. One serious point which worried the project team concerned the payment system. Most of the companies which were enthusiastically pursuing Quality Circles appeared to be in sectors of industry which paid its production employees on measured daywork systems. The project team was worried that the 'group co-operation' concept of Quality Circles might not be compatible with an individual payment by results system.

The bulk of the investigation was therefore concentrated on the clothing industry, a sector of manufacturing industry with many similarities to the footwear industry.

The investigation, which covered some fifteen clothing manufacturers, revealed a high level of success. It also disclosed that consultants had been used in the majority of applications in that industry. There seemed little doubt that Quality Circles could work for Bally, as it had for many other companies, particularly as the company openly encouraged communication with employees at all levels. The only questions which now remained were, 'How would Quality Circles be introduced?' and 'Who would be responsible for the programme?'

The project team's final proposal to senior management outlined three alternative methods of introducing Quality Circles:

1   Using a reputable consultant.
2   Using a Quality Circles Training Package and introducing the concept without any outside help.
3   Attending courses organised by the Industrial Society and introducing Quality Circles without outside help.

Senior management examined the costs of the alternative proposals and decided to introduce Quality Circles with the help of a reputable consultant.

Two consultancies were invited to make presentations and forward proposals and costs to the senior and middle managers who had been responsible for the early work on the project.

The outcome of the presentations was a unanimous decision about which consultancy would help to introduce Quality Circles into Bally and so the scene was set.

The introduction of Quality Circles

An essential rule about Quality Circles is that it is entirely voluntary and this can lead to difficulties, beginning with the selection of the co-ordinator and facilitator. Bob Marston, Personnel Manager and one of the project team who had been responsible for the feasibility study, was pleased to continue his association with Quality Circles as Programme Co-ordinator. This made sense, as the role is entirely compatible with the role of Personnel Manager.

The selection of facilitator can be more difficult. Bally decided that if the introduction was to prove successful a full-time Quality Circles facilitator would need to be appointed. What sort of person would be most suitable for the job? Again the possibilities are endless, ranging from management trainees to mature and experienced supervisors and managers. Bally decided to ask a 24-year-old supervisor who had already indicated his potential in the supervisory field but who had no immediate opportunity of progression. It was felt that a spell of two years in this role would broaden his experience significantly, and in that time some senior supervisory positions would become vacant through retirement. Graham Hadley accepted the invitation and the challenge. An important point here is that, although he was invited to undertake the job, it was stressed that it was an entirely voluntary approach, and that no pressure was involved. Sceptics might argue that simply by asking we were applying pressure. If this is so, then all we can claim is that we did our best to minimise any pressure that was felt.

The next stage was to inform the whole of the management structure and the trade unions of the concept and the company's intentions.

Briefing sessions were arranged in a local hotel and the consultant conducted four sessions lasting approximately one hour each. The delegates at the four sessions were divided thus:

1 Senior and middle management
2 Target Group I (ie department heads and supervisors)
3 Trade union representatives
4 Target Group II

Following the presentations, all the managers and supervisors were asked to think about the concept. Managers were invited to consider whether they would support the concept in their department, and supervisors whether they would like to volunteer to attend the Quality Circles leaders training course.

Of the 44 department heads and supervisors who attended the briefings, 17 supervisors volunteered to attend the company's first Quality Circle leaders course. This presented a problem, as the company only wanted to commence a pilot programme of four circles. Remembering the voluntary concept, another meeting was organised with the 17 volunteers, who were presented with the facts and asked who would prefer to wait for the second phase. The result was seven volunteer leaders to attend the first Quality Circles leaders course.

A three-day course was organised off-site and, although the course was led by the consultant, the co-ordinator and facilitator also ran certain sessions. The course was intended to equip the leaders with the necessary expertise to run their own Circles with the help of the facilitator. It is essential to a successful introduction that the Quality Circles leaders course should go well. We found that the course programme shown below worked exceptionally well, and would recommend the same or a similar model to anyone wishing to introduce the concept.

Day 1   15 September 1982

10 minutes	Introduction
15 minutes	Course objectives
30 minutes	Teaching adults
5 minutes	Introduction to the training material
45 minutes	Introduction to Quality Circles
15 minutes	Coffee
90 minutes	Syndicate work Group 1: Problem solving Group 2: Brainstorming
45 minutes	Syndicate presentation: Group 1
60 minutes	Lunch
45 minutes	Syndicate presentation: Group 2
45 minutes	Analysing problems
15 minutes	Tea
40 minutes	Analysing problems (continued)
20 minutes	Critique
	Conclude Day 1.

Day 2   16 September 1982

10 minutes	Review and update
80 minutes	Working together
15 minutes	Coffee
90 minutes	Syndicate work Group 1: Collecting data Group 2: Management presentation
60 minutes	Syndicate presentation: Group 1

60 minutes	Lunch
60 minutes	Syndicate presentation: Group 2
60 minutes	Meetings, Bloody Meetings (Film)
45 minutes	Dealing with problems in the Circle
15 minutes	Critique
	Conclude Day 2.

Day 3   17 September 1982

15 minutes	Review and update
270 minutes	Quality Circles practical exercise in syndicate group
75 minutes	Lunch
60 minutes	Quality Circles presentations Group 1 Group 2 combined
45 minutes	What next?
15 minutes	Critique
	End of course.

An important aspect of the programme was that it gave the participants the chance not only to learn the problem-solving techniques so vital to successful Quality Circles work, but also to practise their role of trainer to their group. A further important opportunity was that of using all the techniques to solve a real problem they faced as supervisors and of presenting their findings to management.

At the end of the course, participants were asked if they would like to volunteer actually to start a group and, since all seven of the people were so enthusiastic, it was decided to allow all seven to play their part in phase 1. As a result, five Quality Circles commenced immediately, with another two due to start shortly afterwards. All seemed well and we looked forward with confidence to a successful programme. However, five weeks into the programme, an unexpected management reorganisation allowed the facilitator to gain a deserved promotion, and the Quality Circle programme faced a very difficult time. For six weeks the programme continued without a full-time facilitator until Lesley Rudd, formerly an import administration clerk, was appointed facilitator. It should be said that, if the appointment had not been made at that time, Quality Circles might not have continued much longer at Bally, since they do require active support and encouragement in the early stages. They did in fact continue, and the next section deals with the work of some of the Circles which had been set up at Bally in the first phase.

Quality Circles in action

Dereham factory

Initial interest in Quality Circles was very high in our Dereham factory. It is a small factory, with a workforce of about 60 people who all feel a strong sense of identity with their work. The first step was to invite the whole of the section to a presentation which outlined the concept, and after this introduction 17 people volunteered. This was too many for one group and so, in discussion with the facilitator and leader, Ted Rump, who is the section supervisor, a compromise was found which involved starting one group straight away, with a second later in the year.

Dereham have faced and overcome many problems, including a change of manager and losing their original facilitator, but they have overcome this and formed a new commitment to ensure that their meetings take place regularly with the agreement of their new manager, Graham Hadley (our original facilitator). They have chosen the very complex problem of improving the spoils system, both by decreasing the number of spoils and improving the system used. Spoilage is both wasteful and very expensive, so it is an important subject. The problem has involved a great deal of work covering several areas, with plenty of data collection. At times the members have all felt that it was never going to end, but there has always been one who has said, 'We're not going to give up now', and kept the others going. Now they have completed their investigation and given their presentation, which included a poster and cartoon campaign, organised by themselves, to make everyone aware of the cost of a spoil.

During the course of their investigation the Circle found that they could not utilise some of the figures they had collected. This was because they did not relate directly to their area of control, and the focus of Quality Circles is very much on 'putting your own house in order'. Rather than waste the data, however, they passed them to their manager, who has been able to use them to reduce by one third the amount of leather spoiled.

Ted Rump, the supervisor, has found that he does not always have sufficient time to devote to Quality Circles and suggested that we train someone else from the Circle to replace him. The group was involved in this decision and actively agreed. We have trained two of the Quality Circle members, Maxine and Theresa, one of whom will take over Ted's Circle while the other will start a second group. They are now working with Ted until the problem currently being worked on is presented, then Ted will withdraw and become an advisor and source of support to the Circles.

Post machine

There are 30 people in this section, which is supervised by Peter Scott, one of the original leaders trained, who began a Quality Circle in phase 1. Initially he faced many problems with membership – several people volunteered and then dropped out – but he was eventually able to establish a Circle with six members. From the beginning this Circle has met at the same time, on the same day each week. This practice, it soon became apparent, is one of the keys to Quality Circle success because it establishes Quality Circles as part of the work routine, and the pattern is now followed by all of our Circles.

The Circle chose a problem they had with the strengthening tape used in sandal ankle straps. They found it difficult to machine and difficult to trim. Initially the Circle believed that the problem could be solved by using a wider tape, but the data they collected indicated that the problem was not only that the tape was difficult to work with, but also that it did not stick properly to the lining, in which case a wider tape would not help. At this stage the Quality Circle needed specialist advice from the Bally Technical Department. The group invited the relevant person along to a meeting for help and advice. Eventually, and after several trials, a suitable replacement was found.

During this time the Circle felt very frustrated, at one stage having to wait six weeks to get a firm price for a possible new material. Group morale obviously dropped at this stage because they could not understand why a company which should be interested in supplying tape could delay on giving prices. Fortunately, rather than giving up they began to feel that they would not let anyone stop them – they would find out and would finish the problem. They were discouraged by the delay, but this did not cause anyone to say out loud that they felt like giving up, although they admitted it afterwards.

In a less committed group without such a highly motivated leader, the Circle would surely have collapsed, but Peter Scott managed, with careful planning, to think of something to do each week to maintain enthusiasm. The Circle also felt a degree of responsibility to Quality Circles, because they were the nearest to being able to give a presentation to management and, if their Circle had collapsed, a great deal of damage would have been done to the programme. In fact their presentation has acted as a catalyst for other Circles to speed up their work and has also served to create a wider interest in Quality Circles throughout the factory.

After the presentation the Circle moved on to work on a new problem, that of quality of work, and one of the Circle members, Sharen Jones, was then selected by the group and trained to take over the leader role. Peter Scott supported her through the early stages before dropping out to begin another group from the rest of his section.

Purchasing

Fred Bass leads the purchasing department Circle, which has six members. Purchasing covers stores, the office and part of the leather warehouses. Each individual has a different job to do, but the Circle in fact works well, with the members helping each other and sharing experiences even when their tasks are not apparently similar.

The Circle ran into problems soon after it started, firstly because of stock taking, which meant stopping meetings for a couple of weeks, and then the illness of two members of the department, who were not members but whose absence meant that Circle members could not leave the department. This affected progress for several weeks and, together with the Christmas shutdown, meant that the Circle did not meet for a couple of months. With hindsight we can see that we should not have tried to start the Circle until after Christmas. When the meetings did start again the members all felt rather disillusioned because they had been unable to meet, but fortunately this was overcome by establishing a regular meeting time and place.

The Circle chose three problems to work on which would cover everyone's interest: reorganising the stores, reorganising the system for the storage of shoe boxes, and the use of the telex. These problems have been considered separately and in turn, but with work being continued on each topic as another one was considered.

The major topic has been the reorganisation of the stores. This was a problem that the members could see was developing, as workload and the volume of stores was increased, but storage was not. Initially they simply wanted a reorganisation to achieve better workflow and co-ordination. As is very common, however, the data they collected indicated that their initial assumption was not entirely correct, since it became apparent that there was not enough racking available and that, each season bringing with it a new range of shoes, the situation was getting worse.

The group had just finished their plans when their manager realised the situation and spoke to their supervisor. He was interested and enthused by the drawings and studies already completed by the Circle. The next day these were presented to their manager informally, as they had no time to prepare a presentation. The proposals were studied by management to see how quickly they could be achieved, and whether there was sufficient budget to start work straight away. Whilst the stores members concentrated on this, two other topics were considered, one concerning shoe boxes, their storage and positioning in the room. Again whilst work was being done on this, the members heard that there was a plan to reorganise the room. They realised they had to submit their ideas quickly because no one would be very interested in their plans immediately after an expensive reorganisation. Again they made an informal presentation of their idea and plans, which were accepted and incorporated into the new room plan.

They have also collected data on the use of the telex and have found that between them they send 70 per cent of the telexes issued from the company, and yet they are positioned furthest away from the machine.

Problems faced and lessons learned
Our first Quality Circles began in late September 1982. Five were started initially, in the preparation room, post

machine, bottom stock and work study sections and one at our Dereham factory. A sixth started a month later in the purchasing department. Only one Circle, the post machinists, had any problem in attracting sufficient volunteers, but this was overcome by both the facilitator and potential leader speaking again to each of the machinists, but without putting pressure on them.

From this point progress was fairly smooth for some time. There were one or two small problems with one manager not liking so many of his department away from the section at once, but this was overcome with co-operation from all parties by agreeing the most convenient (or least inconvenient) day and time of day.

The facilitator

The first real problem we faced was in fact a serious setback. The company was undergoing a management reshuffle, which ended with promotion for several people, including the Quality Circle facilitator, Graham Hadley. Graham was in two minds as to his best decision: he did not want to drop out of the Quality Circles programme, but the job he was offered was extremely tempting and he eventually decided to take it. Obviously this meant finding a new facilitator, preferably someone from within the company, but unfortunately it is not just a case of finding the right person, but of training them as well, which takes some time. A replacement was found – Lesley Rudd, a clerk from the Imports Department – but because of the Christmas holidays and her training it was February before she could start, which meant our Circles had a two-month period without a facilitator.

This experience confirmed what we were told by our consultant: that the facilitator role is crucial to Quality Circle success, simply because if someone is not around in the early stages to see that meetings happen, the room is free and things get done, then the programme can all too easily begin to crumble. Only one Circle was relatively unscathed by this period because they had already established a set pattern of meetings, were well into their problem, and needed less help. Several of the other Circles needed meetings with our consultant and a new facilitator to re-assess their commitment and rekindle their enthusiasm. Fortunately they were all interested enough to continue, but without the gentle prodding of a facilitator to remind them of their meetings they would soon have stopped having them. Obviously a facilitator leaving is not an everyday occurrence, or the person would not have been chosen in the first place, but it is something to guard against.

The routine

It became clear that a regular meeting pattern is vital, and we now encourage all our groups to have one. Once it is established, Quality Circles become a part of working life, a normal part of the day – in the same way that we know Friday is payday, we know that, say, Thursday at 10.30 is Quality Circle time. One group established a routine from the very beginning and most of the others meant to, but found it easy to say, 'Oh, I'm busy today, we'll have our meeting tomorrow', and so on. An example of this was our bottom stock Circle. The department has a requirement for two supervisors, but one had been sick for three months. This placed substantial extra pressure on the remaining supervisor, the Quality Circle leader, Geoff Lewis. It meant that Geoff was unable to leave his department and had to rely on several of the Circle members to give him extra help. The section's workload was also very heavy at the time and this meant that meetings were suspended for several weeks. This was very depressing for the Circle because they had collected all their data and only needed to prepare a presentation. Their problem was seasonal, and they could see the start of a new season creeping up without their problem being solved.

Fortunately a compromise was arranged. Geoff suggested that the facilitator acted as leader, and that he would arrange for as many members as possible to be made available for the meetings. Obviously this was not ideal, as Geoff had such a vast experience of the department, but with plenty of co-operation, and keeping Geoff completely in the picture, a presentation was prepared, made and accepted. Three members have dropped out of this Circle, one because of retirement, one who got fed up while meetings were suspended and another, Denise, who is pregnant and has now left the company. After she left, however, Denise came back to work especially for Quality Circle meetings because she had been involved from the start. She also took part in the presentation, which shows how committed some people become.

Another aspect of this same problem comes from our work study Circle. For several months the meetings were regular, then for week after week they found two or three members were unavailable for various reasons. The members began to lose interest because, when they did have a meeting, half of it was spent reminding themselves how far they had got. Eventually they decided they would start a new problem, and meet even if everyone was not available.

The real difficulty with not meeting regularly is that no one knows where they are, from the manager to the member, whereas when a routine is established it is usually quite easy to organise your work to allow for a free hour, and everyone soon gets to know that you are not available at a certain time. Circle members also quickly become disillusioned when meetings are cancelled; they are very protective of their Circle and take it personally when this happens. Occasionally, of course, it cannot be helped. Members understand if the workload really is very heavy or a sudden rush job comes through, but they will not accept it for other reasons. On other occasions a heavy workload will prevent a full one-hour meeting, but ten minutes might be possible to review progress. This is much better than having no meeting at all and thereby breaking the pattern. As our consultant told us, habits are difficult to get into but relatively easy to keep up.

In one case, we had a supervisor who began to lose interest because of other work problems and, although individual members understood, as a group they felt let down. His lack of interest led to the cancelling of meetings on any pretext, and frustration began to show, the general feeling being, 'How can we get anything done if we only meet one week in three?' Again we turned to our consultant for advice. Together with the facilitator, he discussed with the supervisor his problems, and established they were not to do with Quality Circles, but rather work pressure that did not give him enough time to enjoy the Circles, and that he still supported the programme. From this we came to an agreement that he would see the first problem through, but that we would train a Circle member to be a leader to help him and then take over. Now this Circle is running very well indeed.

Management support

We have experienced similar problems with other Circles. Leaders need encouragement and support from both the facilitator and their manager. If this support is not strong enough, frustration sets in. They feel they are trying to do something extra in their jobs, and naturally feel that they are doing their best and both the manager and the facilitator must support them, otherwise why should they bother? This is often more a problem of perceptions than anything. It is a problem if the leader feels he is not being given the backing. Often at the same time the manager or facilitator will feel that they are giving enough support. The reality, however, is inside the mind of the leader. Unfortunately, if such problems are not spotted straight away Circle members soon become affected too, because the leader can all too easily begin not to show them enough commitment.

Advertising is another important factor. Everyone likes to know what is going on, whether at home or work, and through advertising what the Circles are doing you achieve two things. One, the rest of the workforce is kept informed and, with luck, interested. Secondly, the Circle members see that what they are doing is appreciated and noted by management. We print a newsletter every six weeks or so to let everyone know what is going on. We include all problems solved, as well as problems being worked on, because someone reading the letter may have an idea everyone else has missed. The newsletter's chief role though is to show that Quality Circles are a part of normal working life at Bally, that management is supporting it throughout the company, and that everyone can be a part of the programme by monitoring progress even if they are not a Circle member.

Management commitment is of course vital, but we have found that management need to do more than just say they are supporting Quality Circles. They have to demonstrate their support. Our whole programme received a tremendous boost after our Managing Director made a special trip from London to attend the opening and a presentation on our second Quality Circle leaders course. His presence was important not only to the people there but to everyone in the company, because he had shown he really was interested and committed. Whenever a manager is asked to attend a meeting to give their opinion or advice, the Circle members and managers always really enjoy the contact, which is not easy to achieve in the normal run of events. A valuable feature of the contact is that they discuss the problem, but are not arguing about it, rather exchanging views and facts in a way that is not possible in normal work routine. John Andersen, our Production Manager, expressed this view after one presentation, saying how much he appreciated the friendly way they were meeting and getting to know each other better, exchanging information and experience, and coming to a joint agreement.

External factors

Another problem we faced involved a leader who became ill and had to spend a number of weeks off work. Even when she returned she was under doctor's orders to avoid stressful situations. This led to her understandable decision to give up the Quality Circle. The problem here was that the rest of the group wanted to continue, but there was no obvious natural leader who could step in immediately. The first thing we decided to do was to talk to the leader to find out whether she was still committed to the concept. If she had said no at this stage, we would have suggested that the group stop meeting, since the whole system can only really work in the long run with support from the supervisor and manager. Fortunately the leader in question was still committed and the decision to quit had been made purely in order to reduce stress. The next stage was to have a discussion with the group to re-establish the members' commitment to it. We then had an informal meeting at which we agreed that the facilitator would become the temporary leader of the group, with the original leader choosing to sit in as a normal member of the Circle. The plan was for this to continue until either the supervisor felt well enough to resume her role, or another member of the group showed the ability and willingness to take on the mantle. In fact the former happened, and with the facilitator's help the group and leader are now progressing well.

It is clear that all our Circles have been faced with a variety of difficulties. Fred Bass's purchasing Circle seems always to be working on a problem that suddenly becomes a crisis. Twice recently his Circle has been collecting data when outside factors have changed a problem to a crisis. On both occasions, as was said earlier, they have managed to get drawings and plans completed in twenty-four hours to present informally to management. Now the department's manager, who was initially uninterested in Quality Circles, sings their praises to everyone, because of the weeks of work that have been saved by the Circle's foresight. The basic message seems to be that there will be difficulties but, if the will is there, they can be overcome to the benefit of everyone.

Most Circles soon learn all the problem-solving skills and enjoy collecting facts; however, the one problem they all face is lack of time. Circles often tend to expect that whatever they want should be made available straightaway. If they ask someone for information they expect it for their next meeting, not appreciating that, although it may be their number one priority, it is not necessarily the other person's. It may be that the other person has other more pressing problems that need to be dealt with first. An example of this came from the post room Quality Circle which, as has already been mentioned, was working on improving a strengthening tape used in sandal bars. The material being used was not easy to work with and gave a poor finish, and working with our technical department they have found a replacement which gives a far superior finish, is stronger and, as a bonus, cheaper. During their investigation they faced extraordinary setbacks, and were kept waiting six weeks for a supplier to give them the price of a certain tape. It was frustrating but they persevered, and whenever one was depressed by the lack of action, another would say 'We're not giving in now.' The leader was also very careful to think of something they could do while they waited, to maintain interest. Finally they found what they needed, and the replacement tape is now being used.

This kind of frustration unfortunately seems to be a part of living in the real world and is therefore something that Quality Circles have to get used to. This does not mean they give up, rather that they keep pushing to get things done but with a recognition that there is no magic wand to make everything happen instantly. It is essential that this recognition is built into the training given to the Quality Circle leaders and members. Similarly, many

Circles have problems that need, for example, help from the maintenance department for a simple repair job or a quote for moving things. Obviously this is extra to the normal maintenance work and has to be fitted in whenever possible, but to Circle members is a five-minute job and they find it difficult to understand why it is not done immediately.

Encouragement

Maybe all Circles, sooner or later, have a setback which makes them say, 'Why bother, why go on when no one is helping us?' Fortunately there always seems to be someone in the Circle who will want to go on and hates to be beaten, and who remotivates the others. The leader, of course, suffers in the same way but can be helped by the facilitator. If this happens it is a dangerous time, when people will feel like dropping out. Nevertheless it is vital that the voluntary principle is adhered to. It is all right to encourage people to continue to look on the positive side, but at all costs it must be clear that the decision rests with the individual concerned. Our drop-out rate has been low. In the first nine months only four people left their groups and a couple of these left the company. To balance, we had three people join in.

The second leader course

Following the success of the initial introduction we decided to run a second Quality Circle leader course. Five people attended, three of whom were members of existing Quality Circles. This was to cover two eventualities: one area where pressure of work on the supervisor meant that he decided with his group to delegate the leader role to two of the members, and the other where the supervisor wanted to give the rest of his section the opportunity to start up in a different group, and so again decided to delegate the leader role in the original Circle. In both situations it is obviously important that the supervisor maintains a watching brief, and is always available to advise and help when required.

On our next leaders course we will be training another Circle member to take over as leader, because some supervisors simply cannot find the time for meetings every week and can be of more help by advising and assisting than by being actively involved.

The future trend at Bally

The Manufacturing Division of the company has already decided to introduce Quality Circles into as many different departments as possible, always remembering that the concept is voluntary. It is envisaged that fifty Circles could be operating by 1986. Of course, this will not happen automatically: it will require continuing hard work and commitment, but at a recent meeting of managers, the programme received a boost which will help to ensure the future success of the programme. On the basis of progress already made, they decided to commit themselves more openly and completely than had been the case up to then and in a five-point statement they agreed:

1 To institute a formal budget for likely Quality Circle innovations and requests;
2 To commit themselves to allowing Quality Circle meetings to be held regularly, whatever the pressures of other work;
3 To make conscious efforts to meet Quality Circle members informally and to demonstrate support for their involvement;
4 To ensure that delays in collecting information for Quality Circles are eradicated;
5 To recognise, both private and publicly, that small problems solved are just as important as big ones.

One trend which developed in the second phase of introduction at the company was that of the Circles being led by a previous Circle member (ie *not* a supervisor or department head). The company sees this trend of Circle ownership as being of great significance and will be encouraging further autonomy in this way.

It is probable that Circles will eventually be started in the other divisions of the company, such as Retail, Marketing and Wholesale, and possible that the concept will be introduced in the Swiss parent company, which has a multinational and multicultural workforce.

Doing the sums:
The toy industry

John Mowat

The toy industry case raises a number of issues which are well worth highlighting. The first is that the Quality Circles approach can work well with virtually any type of employee. A common question is whether the approach works with female staff, especially those who are assumed by some management to work only for the 'pin money'. Quite simply, it does. Experience shows that with any category of staff there will be enough volunteers to get things going, and that often the least likely groups come up with some of the best ideas.

This case history also brings out the question of the resourcing of the programme. Quality Circles cost money. It is important to be clear and explicit about this point, which was recognised, and fully explored, in this situation. Furthermore it was recognised that the investment was a wide-ranging one which included the cost of the time of Circle members which was 'lost', as far as production was concerned, for the one-hour meeting each week. Other ongoing costs which were taken into account included the time of the facilitator and the cost of providing adequate facilities. 'One off' costs included the consultancy fees and also the training material. Not all organisations choose to cost things in this kind of detail, but it is useful that some do since it provides a useful reference point for others. In this case the company was just as precise in its evaluation of the tangible benefits which accrued, and is prepared to admit that the total cost of the programme in the first year, including the 'one off' cost of the consultants and the training material, was quite comfortably paid back during that year by the tangible benefits which came out of the work of the Quality Circles.

There appears to have been a greater emphasis on

producing tangible benefits in this case than in most Quality Circles programmes. An important element of the approach is that it is up to the group to decide which problem it wishes to tackle, and it is a grave mistake for management to impose problems on Circles, since this simply serves to 'steal' the ownership of the groups from the members themselves. In practice many groups actively want to save money for the company and can become despondent and dispirited if they feel they are failing in this quest. Some Circles in the other case studies have demonstrated this phenomenon, but nonetheless it is fatal to break the rule about who chooses the problem to be tackled.

This case also illustrates the possibilities for company, and cultural, variations in introducing the approach. On the American site a number of features were included which might be unacceptable in many companies in Europe, such as the baseball hats which all members are given. The point here is that Quality Circles offer an opportunity for 'customising' the approach to the organisation without impinging on the basic, inviolable principles. If Circles wish to give themselves names, wear hats, to have badges or certificates, no problem is created; the concept is very flexible in this respect. Some organisations even choose to change the name of the approach. In this case the programme has been called 'Employee Action Circles', in Singapore the public service programme is called 'WITS', Work Improvement Teams, and there are many other possibilities for organisations who want to utilise the principles of the approach, but for one reason or another wish to avoid the term Quality Circles.

There is an interesting observation in the text to the effect that 'the lifespan of a Quality Circles programme is much dependent on the number and quality of the problems it tackles, and therefore for some it is potentially short'. Certainly the most likely reason for a Quality Circle to decide to stop meeting is that it feels it is wasting its time, either because 'management won't listen' or because 'we've got nothing to tackle'. As far as this latter point is concerned it is important to stress that Quality Circles can look at opportunities, as well as problems. Given this it is clear that the groups can have an endless life, since it is always possible to make things that little bit better. It can be difficult sometimes to help groups to see that they are entitled to look at opportunities as well as problems, but once the breakthrough is made the concept can rapidly become a part of the normal way things are done in the business.

Toys and games are fast-moving consumer goods in a highly seasonal market where price level and quality standards are essential to success. Manufacturing is high-volume and generally labour-intensive. Any progressive business therefore has to balance a need for good employee relations with a need for employee involvement to improve product quality and to look for ways of reducing costs. Contributions of that kind from employees are crucial to the success of an organisation. But unfortunately all too often employers seem unwilling to take positive action to relate to the workforce in a manner which allows them to make a contribution to the good of the organisation. I was fortunate enough to work with a board of directors who recognised that attention had to be given at senior management level to the improvement of productivity at the manufacturing level. In the first instance it was agreed that the focus should be on one manufacturing site in South Wales. This is a site of some 1,800 people, comprising a manufacturing complex, a distribution operation and the greater part of the company's administration activity, including mainframe computer operations. The manufacturing operation is labour-intensive and the majority of the workforce is female. Labour is heavily unionised and the company operates within a fairly traditional UK industrial relations climate. The terms of reference set down initially by the senior management of the company to look for improvements in productivity were broad.

The introduction of Quality Circles
It was believed that productivity improvement would stem from the workforce gaining a better understanding

of the organisation and the factors which affected it, from improved standards of supervision, improved methods of communication and improved workforce involvement. Achievement of these objectives, it was thought, would lead to improvements in quality and efficiency and to a lowering of scrap and re-work costs. Some research was carried out to establish the most appropriate vehicle to achieve these objectives, and Quality Circles was chosen as one suitable project, to be complemented by a programme leading to improved supervisory training and to an improved and structured plan of communication throughout the whole workforce. A number of large companies with experience of Circles programmes, including May and Baker and ITT, were visited by representatives of the company in order to see at first hand the practical experience of Quality Circles introduction and operation, and also to examine the reasons for failure where failure had occurred. Subsequently a series of consultancies offering Quality Circles programmes training were interviewed by the company, and one of them was appointed to introduce a Quality Circles programme into the Welsh factory site. The appointment was made subject to some closely-defined parameters being agreed. In the first instance it was recognised that Quality Circles would only succeed if there was a total commitment from the most senior managers and directors of the company. This required presentations to be made to the senior executives and a commitment to follow up on an individual basis any of this group who expressed reservations about the approach.

The second prerequisite was to establish and agree a budget for expenditure embracing the cost of consultants, the cost of training materials, the cost of provision of Quality Circles facilities, the cost of lost labour time during Quality Circles activity, and the cost of lost production, if any, during Quality Circles activity. Let us qualify for a moment those prerequisites.

Proper facilities must be provided. Quality Circles

53

need somewhere to meet, preferably not a shared facility, since they need a reasonable degree of privacy for their meetings. They require furnishings to include filing and storage cupboard space for Quality Circles materials. The company, if it has not already got an enlightened philosophy, must be prepared to grant time off during normal working hours for Circle members to take part in meetings, and must be prepared to allow its specialists in industrial engineering and other specialist functions to give time and support to Quality Circles to help them as required. Most important, it must be prepared to communicate with the workforce, perhaps giving more information about company finance, competitive activity, investment philosophy etc., than it has done in the past. If a suggestion scheme exists, a decision must be made as to whether the improvement proposals made by Circles will be rewarded or reward-free. And finally, if production is affected as a result of Circle members leaving their workstations during working hours to go to their Circle meetings, the company must be prepared to accept such a loss or to meet any increased costs to make up any production deficiencies.

All these prerequisites were considered by the directors and senior managers of the company and the following points were agreed. Firstly, a Quality Circles meeting room would be provided, with proper storage facilities. Secondly, paid time off would be allowed on the basis of one hour per Quality Circles member per week, and any production deficiencies resulting from this downtime would be accepted. Many of the workforce have productivity incentives and so it was further agreed that the personal average incentive rate of Quality Circle members would be paid in addition to base rate, for the hour of the meeting. Thirdly, industrial engineering and other specialist or technical functions would be encouraged to support Circles where help was solicited, and fourthly, the company, bearing in mind its responsibilities to shareholders, would, subject where necessary to directors' approval, be prepared to increase the amount of information it had previously released about the company's business and finances. As regards the suggestion scheme it was decided that Quality Circles would and indeed should be reward-free, and that any idea which appeared in the suggestion scheme after being discussed by a Quality Circle would be disallowed. However, any suggestion in the scheme which was recorded as entered before consideration by a Quality Circle would continue to be eligible for suggestion scheme awards if adopted.

Preparations

With these commitments a timetable was established for the implementation of a pilot Quality Circles programme, with the intention of establishing three Circle groups only so that they could be given the specific consultant and in-house attention needed to ensure success, which should in its turn encourage an extension of Circle activity. In the first instance, the timetable, as shown on p. 56, required a series of presentations to all levels of management down to and including every first-line supervisor. These presentations were supported by a continuing process of follow-ups with the sceptics who emerged during the presentation sessions. In addition, all the trade union representatives in the company were given the same presentation and the same opportunity to address questions to directors of the company in order to satisfy themselves in particular that any Quality Circles activity would not be allowed to cut across established trade union negotiation and consultation procedures, and that Quality Circles would not be allowed to pursue subjects which the trade unions and the company would normally consider to be within the established lines of industrial relations and communication.

This series of presentations took place over a four-week period, during which time a Quality Circles facilita-

Timetable for implementation of pilot Quality Circles

Key activities	Day / Month	5/6	12/6	19/6	26/6	3/7	10/7	17/7	24/7	31/7	7/8	14/8	21/8	28/8	4/9	11/9	18/9	25/9
1	Consult senior executives and outline planning.	▓																
2	Design and hold presentations to senior management.			▓														
3	Present to departmental managers, supervisors and trade union reps.				▓	┊ ┊												
4	Identify potential Circle areas and leaders.					▓												
5	Prepare and hold leader training courses.						▓	*										
6	Prepare and present to potential Circle areas.							▓	▓									
7	Start Circles.								▓									
8	Prepare monitoring and control procedures.											▓	↑					
9	Hold support group meetings.	*	*	*	*	*	*	*	*			*	*	*	*	*	*	*
10	Review progress.					*								*				*

FACTORY SHUT

56

tor was appointed from senior line management. It was agreed, furthermore, that this facilitator would have the full-time support, in the initial Quality Circles programme, of a training officer from the company's Personnel Department. These two men received advance training from the management consultant before actively involving themselves in the presentations, particularly those aimed at first-line supervision and the trade union representatives. Once the communication cycle was completed, sectional meetings were held with every member of the workforce and presentations were made by the facilitator and his assistant, together with the supervisor of the section being addressed. From these meetings volunteers were sought to take part in Circle activity. At the same time volunteers were sought from the supervisory group to accept responsibility as Quality Circles leaders. In all cases, involvement in Circles activities, whether as a leader or a member, was totally voluntary.

Sufficient Circles leader volunteers came forward from the first-line supervisory group to plan for two Circle leader courses, each to be of three days' duration. The first of these courses was to be run by the consultant engaged to support the establishment of Circles, assisted by the company staff responsible for Circle activity, and in the second course the company staff carried out the training under the general supervision of the consultant. Following completion of the three-day training the volunteers were again asked if they wished to go ahead, return to their workgroups and seek volunteers to establish a Quality Circle. At this stage one or two supervisors said that they were not ready to undertake such a responsibility, but the majority volunteered to involve themselves actively in Circle development.

It then became necessary to timetable the introduction of Circles by discussion with that group of supervisors. This was felt to be important so as not to demotivate anyone who, though anxious to run a Circle programme, may not be able to start a Circle immediately. The trained supervisors therefore selected amongst themselves three leaders for the first phase. These nominees were supported by the in-house facilitator in making presentations in their own work area about the purpose of Quality Circles. In every case there were more volunteers than places, and again it was left to the workgroup to agree amongst themselves which of the volunteers would join the Quality Circles and which would stand down to await further Circle development. The reason for such an enthusiastic response is perhaps best summarised by some of the comments from the volunteers.

'I do the job, but no-one ever asks me if I could do it differently or better.'

'I see things coming through which I think are below quality standard, but the Quality Inspector accepts them and doesn't tell me why.'

'I try to give ideas to my supervisor but nothing ever seems to come of them.'

'With 1,800 people in the factory, it's no wonder that you never get a chance to talk to me about my thoughts.'

'I think we waste money doing this, but presumably it's OK because the company doesn't seem to want to change it.'

Getting the Circles into operation

The first three Circle groups having been selected, training began under the control of the company facilitator. Each Circle group took one hour per week to learn the basic skills to make them effective Circle contributors. This training was specifically related to their work situation, as distinct from non-work-related theoretical exercises, and as a result, concurrent with the training, the Circles were encouraged to identify a first project and to look for proposed solutions to the chosen problem for presentation to their manager at the end of the training period. Perhaps the greatest initial difficulty here was to guide the Circles into identifying problems for correction which were directly concerned with the production operation, as distinct from being welfare points, such as 'the canteen', 'the state of the toilets', etc. This meant that the facilitator had to draw on his management experience to encourage people to look more closely and specifically at the work they were employed to do on the production line.

Let us turn for a moment and look at the initial reactions from the workforce at large, because so far we have only examined the enthusiasm of those who volunteered to pursue Circle activity. Inevitably the proposal for introduction of Quality Circles was met with a fair degree of disbelief and cynicism. There are always managers, perhaps particularly the older senior supervisors, who have come up from the shopfloor, who will say, 'We have heard it all before,' and 'The shopfloor will not be interested.' In fact, as we have already said, shopfloor reaction was very positive. This manager resistance to tapping ideas from the shopfloor tended to come where fears that the creation of Circles would constitute a threat to the authority and status of the supervisor. On the union side, as we have already mentioned, there was strong reservation, firstly that Circles would circumvent their authority. It had to be made very clear that Circles would not discuss any items normally the prerogative of company union discussion, and equally it was important that Circles would not be allowed to bypass the normal managerial chain of communication and of command. Another typical early question prompted largely by the unions was, 'What's in it for us?', but the company's answer was consistently the same, that is, that any workforce contribution that could actively contribute to profitability secures employment and the necessary funds to make genuine labour negotiations and satisfactory payrates possible. Another of the problems which manifested itself was that of the individual workgroups consistently 'pointing the finger' at others and blaming them for the creation of poor-quality products. Assembly argued that the Plastic Moulding Shop was supplying badly moulded parts – 'It's not our fault they won't go together.' Packaging complained that Assembly was not doing its job properly – 'It's not our problem that the packaging looks untidy.' The company had to combat these comments by explaining the benefits of getting groups to identify their own problems, instead of freely blaming others for difficulties.

There was also a problem with the Circle groups themselves, the problem of over-enthusiasm and over-ambition. Some Circles attempted to develop projects beyond their capability, and it was necessary to drum in, 'Think small, grow big' to all of the Circle members. Here it is worth touching on the need for effective Circle control, especially in the initial period. We have already said that the company facilitator was responsible for supporting the first-line supervisor in the training and development of their Circle group. In real terms this meant that, for the first three months of Circle activity, the facilitator would attend each and every Circle meeting to ensure that training was being adequately provided by the supervisor, and that the Circles were applying their newly-learned skills in an objective manner. Equally the facilitator, as an experienced production manager, was able during the course of Circle meetings to explain and expand on points being raised about which the Circle members had insufficient knowledge, and where he did not have such knowledge he was able to act as a catalyst, encouraging the supervisor to go to Industrial Engineering and other technical departments to ask for support and assistance. Whilst in some cases there was an initial resistance to providing such assistance, generally speaking technical departments were very willing to visit the Circle groups to discuss with them problems arising or to clarify with them any points of misunderstanding. Finally as a control, the Circles were each required at the end of each one-hour meeting to produce a brief summary minute of the content of

their meeting, this minute being circulated to the departmental manager, to technical managers, and to the
Personnel Director of the company, who had been
nominated to maintain an overall control of the Circle
programme. The purpose of this minute was essentially
twofold. Firstly it was a means of communicating to
interested parties what the Circle was involving itself in,
and secondly it ensured that the Circle did not pursue a
problem or problem area which the company might have
already considered and would not want the Circle to
pursue any further.

The first results

Thanks to these controls and to the support of the
company facilitator, the first Circle groups took about
twelve weeks to achieve their first successes. In one case,
an annual saving of £12,500 was identified in recycling
cardboard work-in-progress containers, instead of
throwing them away. In another case an even more
substantial saving was identified in the labelling
department, where the group significantly reduced waste
and increased labour efficiency. However, one of the
initial Circles also experienced its first failure. A project
they had pursued with considerable vigour was found at
the end to bring such small savings that it destroyed the
enthusiasm of the group, and a great deal of concerted
effort had to be put behind re-forming the Quality Circle
in this section.

Another point which became very apparent at the end
of the first twelve weeks was the real amount of time that
both the facilitator and the seconded training officer
were having to give to the Circle activity. In essence they
devoted 100 per cent of their work effort to the development of the Quality Circles programme at the expense of
some of their other responsibilities. However, it was
encouraging to find that, at the expense of some of their
domestic responsibilities, Circle members were devoting
time at home during evenings and weekends to examin-

ing the problems that they were dealing with and to preparing for presentations of their solutions to line management. Without prompting and without assistance, each of the Circles produced a very high standard of visual aids to support their presentations, and despite extreme nervousness every single member of the Circle group in each case insisted on playing some part in the presentation to their manager.

On an ongoing basis it is interesting to note that Circles quickly become close teams with an obvious interdependence, though this led to another problem. When a Circle member left the group, the rest of the team sometimes found it difficult to accept a new member even where there was no shortage of volunteers. Equally in production environments where flexibility and movement of labour is important, Circle continuity can become difficult, and in one or two cases, as our Circle experience developed, we found this disadvantageous to the confidence of the Circle group. Circles need stability. They need to feel the confidence of the company and of their managers in what they do, and they certainly need the confidence of a co-ordinator whom they can turn to at any time for advice and assistance.

The American programme

Quality Circles seem increasingly to be attracting an international interest, and, at the same time as the programme so far described for the UK operating plant was being introduced, a programme was being introduced in another manufacturing unit in North America. Again a unionised environment, this production operation has a mixed ethnic workforce reflecting the varied nationalities of the community in which it is sited, and again a significant proportion of its labour is female. In very many respects the introduction of the Quality Circles programme to this factory parallels the work done in the UK, although there are some interesting variations.

One important one was the establishment of a Steering Committee, consisting of company general and technical management as well as the chairman of the unions represented in the company. He was invited to join this Steering Committee to avoid any accusation or recrimination about the Circles being means for 'union-busting'. This Steering Committee meets on a regular, planned basis to review collectively reports coming from each of the Circle meetings. The group ensures that full support is given to the Circle projects by both line managers and working colleagues, and it also helps the Circles to direct themselves towards projects of maximum benefit to the business and not to waste time on projects which the company sees as being less relevant. In establishing such a committee, it becomes possible for the co-ordinator, who is also part of that committee group, to feed back to the Circles reasons for certain management decisions being taken, and this has been found to be a very effective means of improving communication flow.

A second difference from the Welsh experience is perhaps culturally influenced. It concerns the identity which Quality Circles generate. Each group, for example, has given its Quality Circle a name. 'Solution finders', 'Super-challenge', 'Inner Circle', 'Operation Seek and Solve', 'Hickey pickers', 'Crusaders for Service', are some of the examples of the names which the members themselves have chosen to emphasise to other members of the workforce the purpose for which they have been formed. To reinforce this, once the Circle member has completed the training he or she is given, and usually chooses to wear, a baseball cap with 'Employees' Action Circles' emblazoned across the front. This has a very practical value in that, in a large workstation, non-Circle members are able to identify easily and quickly Circle members whom they can approach with problems which they believe the group may have the opportunity to address.

Interestingly, the American Circles programme has taken the principles of the concept one stage further than we have in the UK in that, after completion of the first twelve months of activity, a Quality Circle has been formed of the Quality Circles leaders themselves, and this group has been very effective in addressing many of the different problems and opportunities which relate to Circles and Circle activity. This group meets monthly, and is currently working on advanced leader training, on improved methods of training for new members to existing Circles, on co-ordinating and examining means for overcoming problems experienced by existing Circles in their projects, and on examining ways to improve the effectiveness of Circle meetings. In addition the continuing enthusiasm for Circle activity in this operation is supported by the formation of a local association in the geographic area, which associates with the International Association of Quality Circles. Partly as a result of this, the American site has doubled its Quality Circles operation in recent months, and has an active programme of problems outstanding for consideration. This is a welcome situation, because the lifespan of a Quality Circles programme is much dependent on the number and quality of the problems it tackles, and therefore for some is potentially short. If this is the case, the alternatives have to be built on the positive employee attitudes that Circles develop.

The way ahead

Circles generate more effective communication and participation, and workforce attitudes improve with a clearer understanding by the workforce of the problems that a company faces. Equally a company can be significantly more sympathetic to a workforce with which it associates closely, as is the case, in our experience, where Quality Circles exist. The problem which as managers we must face for the future is to establish how to maintain the consultative and participative style of management that a workforce comes to recognise in a Circle environment. We have to acknowledge that the effort that has gone and continues to go into making Circles a success must not be lost.

The corporate culture: Blackwell's

David Young and Tony Graham

The Blackwell's case is a good illustration of a point often made about Quality Circles, that it needs to be introduced as a coherent part of a managerial philosophy. It is particularly interesting to note the build-up to the introduction of the concept, involving as it did significant change and development affecting the whole of the organisation. This is not, of course, to say that all this was done with Quality Circles in mind. As was stated in the case history, Quality Circles is a link in a chain, an important one, but a link nonetheless; it is not an end in itself. If Quality Circles is viewed as an end in itself it becomes much more simple and straightforward, but also, unfortunately, much more likely to fail. Much of the complexity of the approach stems from the fact that it needs to fit within the rest of the organisation. Many companies have introduced programmes 'to see what happens' or because 'it sounds like a sensible idea, so why not have a go?' One very useful contribution this case can make, therefore, lies in showing the value of thinking about the concept in the context of the whole organisation, and of making conscious decisions about the order of priorities in developing the overall health and effectiveness of the organisation. One suspects that without the work that was done in the years building up to the introduction of Quality Circles in Blackwell's, the approach would not have made as much sense as it appears to today.

A number of other interesting details emerge from the case. The first concerns the group which did not start and the one which stopped meeting after a couple of months. From the outset it must be borne in mind that ultimately it is the people themselves who make the decision about whether they want to start or continue. The point at issue here, however, is the reason given in the history for not wishing to begin and continue. In both cases it was that the members were unable to see any worthwhile problems to work on. Even if this is a reasonable assessment, it is somewhat disappointing when a group does not see the opportunities available for making things even better, but then again it is maybe not too surprising, since for most people the whole concept is very new and unusual. In most organisations members of staff are not expected to solve problems, let alone look for opportunities, and in any company of any size there will be some people who find it difficult and alien to think and behave in this way. In circumstances such as those outlined in the case history, therefore, there is no immediate answer. The decision of the workgroup must be respected, but the door must very consciously be left open. It is no bad idea to suggest a formal review of the situation in three or six months to see if views have changed in the light of the experience of other Quality Circles in the organisation.

Such occurrences also emphasise the importance of creating an environment within which people do look for opportunities, even though things may be perfectly satisfactory at the moment. A key to success lies in our ability to encourage people never to be satisfied, but always to be looking for a way of making things even better. Acceptance of the status quo, especially in the turbulent world of today, is actually a recipe for falling behind, and the more staff at all levels understand their role in preventing this the more safe, secure and prosperous is likely to be their company in the long run. If a significant number of workgroups within an organisation reacted in the same way as the two in this case, it would signal at the very least a need for a review of roles and expectations at different levels and also an objective assessment of the management style of the company. Most people are creatures of their environment, both at work and outside, and the way they react says something about their perceptions of how they are treated and how they are expected to behave.

The second interesting feature of this case is the use of part-time facilitators. It is quite usual, at the outset, to find a number of middle managers who are interested in taking on the role, and to have such people investing a half or one day a week looking after one or two groups is a useful way of managing the load of resourcing the programme. Furthermore, it helps to spread knowledge about the concepts in practice and also commitment to the approach. The danger, of course, lies in the demands of the mainline job. If short-term requirements put pressure on a part-time facilitator the Quality Circle can receive less back-up than it requires, especially during the first six months or so. This point is raised in other case histories and is important because there is no doubt that the role of facilitator is crucial to success in Quality Circles. Blackwell's, as is explained in their article, have decided to make it a part of the line responsibility of one manager to ensure that their groups do not suffer in this way. The ideal solution is probably to have a full-time facilitator backed up as needed by other interested part-timers. There are, however, many feasible ways of managing the resource requirement, and the only essential guideline is that trained resources are deployed and that the support is provided for as long as the Quality Circles themselves need and want it.

The third point to highlight is the expectations that many groups have of themselves. The case history mentions that some groups became despondent and frustrated because the problems they were working on and solving were not saving large amounts of money. This is not an unusual feature, but it is one that requires careful handling. One of the core principles of the Quality Circles approach is that the groups themselves choose the problems they wish to tackle. This gives them the ownership of the activity and prevents it being just another management-owned initiative. Against this background it is interesting to note how often groups become concerned if they are not generating tangible savings. It does seem that many groups have a real need to be able to count their contribution, which sometimes causes difficulties, for not every problem tackled will be readily quantifiable in its impact. One multinational company with a thriving Quality Circle programme has kept a detailed log of projects tackled and successes achieved and, out of over three hundred substantial problems which have been worked on, less than 10 per cent have had a clearly identifiable financial payback. It is essential, since this will be the likely pattern in many companies, that management do all they can to show that success is not only counted in direct money savings, indeed that it is the process of involvement and the way the groups work that counts. This point is relevant to a number of the case histories in this book, and management will do well to communicate their expectations clearly and consistently, especially during the first one to two years of their programme.

In the past twenty years much has been written about motivation and management style that is heavily value-laden and uses terms so emotive that it alienates many managers. Much the same language has been used in discussions on Quality Circles. In practice, the only critical judgement is a belief that people doing work in a certain area are well-placed to contribute to improving that work and that given the opportunity they will wish to do so. If you have created a climate amongst managers and supervisors which also subscribes to this belief, then you are in business.

Quality Circles is compatible with almost any corporate structure. However, it must be viewed in a total context of style and employee (including management) skills.

The use of Quality Circles in this way is exemplified in the Mail Order Division of B. H. Blackwell Ltd. The company employs some 600 people in bookselling, both retail and to libraries. It is privately owned, has a worldwide reputation for excellence and is commercially successful. The Mail Order Division employs 196 people and sells books to Academic Institutions in 140 countries.

The background
To put Quality Circles in context within the Mail Order Division of Blackwell's, however, it is necessary to go back to 1977. The problems being faced by the Division at that time included reducing volume, poor relationships between departments and individuals and low morale, and it was at this time that the new Divisional Director, Miles Blackwell, saw the need for a new approach aimed at improving overall effectiveness. He recognised both

the long-term nature and the complexity of the task, and committed himself to following through the process he initiated. Early in 1978 meetings were held with managers and supervisors to announce and introduce a revised organisation structure and to discuss the style of working which was to be encouraged in the Division. This was followed by a memorandum from Miles Blackwell to all staff, an important document which is reproduced below.

From: RMB

DIVISIONAL AIMS

At the recent organisation structure meeting, I mentioned that I believe we should be trying to develop into a management team which has four main aims. I have been asked to put these on paper and circulate them in the Division. They are as follows:

1   Everyone should have a say in the decisions which affect them, so that we only make these decisions when they have been well talked over and given a proper airing. At the same time, when a decision has been made, it will be binding on us all and everyone must do his best to support it and make it happen.

2   Everyone involved in the Division should not only do the best he can himself but also be confident that his colleagues will be trying to do the same. Bearing in mind that we all have our strengths and weaknesses, we can work together and succeed far better as a team. Difficulties or problems are generally best dealt with by joint discussion leading to joint action.

3   Each of us should consciously try to improve his own performance because by doing so he will

not only help himself but also the whole team as well – the team from which we will all draw strength and assistance.

4 Everyone should have the chance of using his talents to their fullest extent and we must work together to make the best of ourselves and each other.

The upward climb

The statement was met with a combination of interest, excitement, doubt and scepticism, and there was a real need to find mechanisms to help it to happen. Four main methods were used; firstly, the deployment of inter-departmental project groups to work on a range of important topics of practical relevance to the Division. Those involved in the groups came from all levels in the organisation as was appropriate to the task in hand. The groups were given additional assistance as necessary and access to a wide range of information and resources. The second main thrust was the development, through a senior level project group, of a radical new organisation which changed the flow of work from a series of linked functional 'drainpipes' to, as far as possible, an inte-grated geographic area concept, where the whole task of servicing the customers' requirements was undertaken by a section dedicated to the customers in that particular geographic area.

The third mechanism used was a major training and development programme involving supervisors and managers. This focused on two areas, of which the first was the interpersonal skills which would be needed to work successfully within the Division aims. The Divi-sional Director also foresaw a period of growth and increasing technical complexity which would necessitate improved performance in management and supervision, whereas in the past the focus had been on traditional bookselling skills. The second area of training and development was, therefore, the development of relevant managerial and supervisory skills in both theory and practice. The fourth innovation was the introduction of briefing groups to ensure a rapid and effective transfer of information within the organisation, especially between different levels. Though it is often claimed to effect a two-way flow of communication, it was recognised that the briefing group system has limitations in this respect. It was felt, however, that it represented the best available mechanism, and would at least ensure that the vital task of disseminating important information was tackled in an organised and systematic way. This goal was achieved very successfully. Much time and effort was also put into trying to encourage a genuine two-way flow of communication, and though some success was achieved in this it was by no means complete.

Progress

By 9 July 1979 much had happened; there was still considerable scepticism, but many people at all levels were beginning to grasp the opportunity. A progress report written on the above data examined, amongst other things, what had been achieved so far. This section of the report is reproduced below.

> *What we have achieved so far*
> It is always more difficult to generate change and tangible benefits when volume is declining. This is especially so in a company which takes as humanitarian an approach to its staff as does Blackwells. Despite this several major benefits have been achieved to date. These include:
> – Since 30/6/78 the manning level in the Division has been reduced by 38 full-time employees (FTEs) by non-replacement or voluntary severance. A new organisation has been designed, based on geographic areas. This was done by the senior managers in the Division working as a team. There is an unprecedented commitment to make it work.

– The first stage of the physical relocation (involving 1,600 pieces of furniture and 185 staff) has been completed on schedule with minimum disruption of normal work.

– The Bibliography section has been reorganised so that Bench and VDU bibliographers can get themselves into shape for the second stage of the reorganisation.

– The Division has a communication policy that is uniform and reinforces the role of the supervisors and managers as spokesmen for the firm. It was created by the people in the Division with the backing of the Personnel Director.

– Many, though not all, of the managers and supervisors have become more responsible, more willing and able to work together and better at the process of managing.

– Quality of service, work scheduling and productivity control systems have been developed and implemented by the different management groups. There is a high degree of ownership of these systems among the managers and supervisors. Weekly meetings are held in the areas to plan the work for the week ahead, to get the best use out of the hours available, and to serve the customer well. The sections are better controlled through these systems, productivity levels are improving in most areas (see below) as is customer service. There is still some way to go, but a solid start has been made which will form the basis of future improvements. It is interesting to consider the progress made in each geographic area over the past four months since the planning and control systems were devised.

The report then goes on to list details of the improvements in both productivity and service which led to the overall result recorded above.

These are all important and positive benefits. One defect in our performance to date, however, has been that we have not paid enough attention to inter-divisional relations. We have been so immersed in the programme that we have tended to forget that others may not share our views. This has resulted in a number of misconceptions which are damaging to the programme. Since we have to live with other people's perceptions, however erroneous, we must make sure that we do not fall into this trap again. We must do our best to clarify our stance on key issues and ensure that other divisions understand our reasoning.

The achievements

After several more months of consolidation of the new structure and philosophy the true benefits of two years' effort really began to show, and through 1980 and 1981 great strides were made, including the development of the divisional management group into a really effective decision making body, building on the training that they had received. They not only understood the need for consensus, but were able to achieve it and to accept the requirement for 'cabinet' responsibility. Problems were tackled in an organised manner by a team which had become mutually supportive, and which had overcome its previous difficulties of goal and role confusion.

The reorganisation of departments into customer groupings rather than functional units enabled staff to develop greater awareness of their customers' needs, and an insight into the real possibilities of the team concept. Area supervisors were able to control all aspects of the service given to a specific group of customers, and involve the workforce in the planning and control of throughput.

Jobs were redesigned to allow more variety of tasks and to build flexibility. An in-depth training programme was devised to enable staff to become skilled in other roles, and to progress through job grades accordingly. Career progression through this kind of job-enrichment was one of the central factors in the new structure. It served to emphasise that technical competence offered a way forward in its own right, and could be developed separately from managerial skills.

Finally, supervisors and staff alike developed the knowledge and confidence to resolve their own problems, and the project group approach to interdepartmental problems gained greater acceptance. Exception routines were minimised, workflow improved and significant increases in productivity were realised, for example the number of full-time employees reduced by 31 per cent between 1977/78 and 1981/82 while productivity increased by 20 per cent during the same period. Participative supervision encouraged the workforce towards higher levels of achievement, and gave them greater ownership of what they were doing.

During 1982 the Division reached a stage where the original objectives had been largely achieved. It was a highly effective, profitable concern and, when an upturn in business began during 1982, it was well-equipped to respond. Although natural wastage had substantially reduced the overall manning level, the majority of operational staff had lived through the reorganisation process and formed the basis of a mature workforce. There was a healthy climate, where people displayed enthusiasm and commitment, and were consistently striving to improve their performance. The path had not always been easy, indeed the process was one of 'three steps forward, two steps back'; some project groups had failed, while some had been very successful. A few supervisors had found it too difficult to adapt their style and had left the company on a voluntary and assisted basis, but most had responded to the training and development, and indeed to the new opportunity. The next step which was needed was to broaden the base of involvement and to give the opportunity for all staff to participate. The workforce now contained many highly skilled, self-motivated personnel who had become accustomed to change and who also had high expectations. They sought involvement and needed to feel that there would be an ongoing opportunity to contribute to the development of the Division. Following a detailed investigation of the different possibilities, it was decided that the next logical step would be to introduce a Quality Circles programme, since this appeared to be a natural extension of the philosophy which had already gained wide acceptance.

Quality Circles at Blackwell's

The programme was carefully constructed and involved the use of the same consultant who had helped with the Organisation Development programme and who had had extensive experience of the Quality Circles approach. Stage 1 was to give a series of introductory talks aimed at describing the approach and outlining the plan of introduction in Blackwell's. From the outset, commitment from top management was both sought and given. Miles Blackwell in particular reinforced his longstanding commitment to the managerial philosophy within which Quality Circles can flourish, and to the new Quality Circles programme in particular. The Quality Circles leader course was over-subscribed with volunteers, and at the end of the three-day course everyone who attended still wanted actually to start a group. In practice this caused a small problem, since there were not enough trained facilitators to support this number of groups starting together. All those who had been trained, therefore, were involved in deciding the plan of introduction, which took the form of three phases spread over a six-month period.

The Blackwell's Quality Circles programme at the time of writing is well into its second year. Currently eight groups are active, involving some fifty to sixty staff out of the 196 staff in the Division. The introduction of the approach into the organisation was assisted by all the work which had been done in the years before, but even so it was not all plain sailing. In one area where the supervisor offered to begin a group, there were not enough volunteers to make it possible. This was not due to any particularly negative attitude, rather that the workgroup in question felt that they did not have any problems that were substantial enough to make it worthwhile. Although disappointing in that it settled for the status quo rather than improvement, it was the decision of the group and as such was respected.

Another group started enthusiastically but then found it increasingly difficult to find compelling projects to work on. Again they concluded that they had no problems as such, and so decided to stop meeting, at least for the time being. Apart from these two instances the groups which began are still all in existence.

Problems solved

A wide range of topics have been discussed in the Quality Circles and many problems have been tackled. One group commissioned some further training for itself as its first problem. Their reasoning was that it would give them a better understanding of the computer system which affected every part of their work, and that this would lead to an improved ability to identify and solve other problems that they had. Another group was concerned about inconsistencies in the receipt of advance information about forthcoming books from publishers. This is an essential ingredient in the service this group gives to its customers and so they designed a questionnaire, arranged to go to a Book Trade Fair and conducted a survey of the publishers who were present. The results were startling. For example, about half the publishers were not aware of the existence of this particular section or did not know that advance information was required.

As a result of this information the Quality Circle was

able to devise an action plan and present it to management. It was accepted and many of the issues are now solved or are being solved. Another Quality Circle has found a way of reducing the number of very expensive books which have to be either returned to the publisher or reduced in price because eventually the customer decides he does not want them.

Lessons learned

The Blackwell's Quality Circles programme has not led to huge savings, but this was not expected nor was it the main reason for introducing the concept. Interestingly this, at one stage, made some of the groups begin to feel that they were failing because their solutions were not saving large amounts of time or money. It was necessary to brief some of the leaders and facilitators again so that they could reinforce the message that success did not have to be measured in thousands of pounds.

From the start of the programme a number of trained facilitators have been used to support the programme. Typically a facilitator has looked after one group, or at the most two, and has fitted this work around the requirements of the rest of the job. This worked well for a time, but for some facilitators this became quite problematical as the pressures of work in their line role increased. In one or two cases the time spent by the facilitator began to become rather intermittent, and this seemed to reflect in the performance of the Quality Circles themselves. Those groups which were affected began to miss meetings, and their motivation and commitment faltered on occasions. To ensure that the appropriate amount of back-up is given on a regular basis, the task of co-ordinating and facilitating has recently been agreed as a formal part of the job of one of the managers. This will help to ensure that the groups do meet regularly and with the required help as needed, provided by a combination of the original part-time facilitators and the new co-ordinator/facilitator.

Summary

In the Mail Order Division of Blackwell's, Quality Circles is a link in a chain. The chain is the way we manage and our philosophy of doing so. Quality Circles is a vital part of it for, without a means of enabling all staff to become involved, any such management style would be 'like a sounding brass or a tinkling cymbal', all wind and no pitch!

Getting going:
Bank of America

Jean Hills

The Bank of America case, coming as it does from a service industry, clearly gives the lie to the commonly-held view that Quality Circles are only relevant in manufacturing industry. In fact, there is currently a tremendous growth of programmes in banks, insurance companies, government departments and other such settings, and the approach fits these environments just as well as it does any other where the culture and style of the organisation is compatible.

An interesting point about this study concerns their employee suggestion scheme, 'Ideas in Action'. Unlike some organisations, they encourage Quality Circles to submit their solutions as a group and share the monetary award equally. A Circle recommendation is eligible for entry only if it has already been approved by the management to whom the presentation had been made. The system seems to work well here, although the majority of Circles in the bank consider recognition from their managers to be a more fitting reward, and many elect not to submit their solutions to the scheme. Whilst the two programmes run in harmony for this organisation, it should not be assumed, however, that such a system will be either appropriate or, indeed, welcomed in every setting. In a number of organisations which have set up programmes for Quality Circles to put forward their ideas to suggestion schemes, qualifying groups have rejected the opportunity on the grounds that it would 'spoil things' or that 'we are not in it for this kind of reward'. It is neither right nor wrong to allow Quality Circles access to such rewards, but organisations should be careful to think through the implications of any decisions they make in this respect. It is all too easy to assume that staff will 'jump for the jellybeans' at every opportunity and on this basis to rush into setting up such a system. Beward Theory X! The main reasons why people join Quality Circles are to satisfy needs for recognition and achievement, and there is a danger that introducing money could dilute the recognition aspect. It would be possible, for example, for people to rationalise that management would assume the only reason staff were getting involved was to get at the money. If this were the case, recognition could be seriously devalued and one of the most potent motivations would be impaired. This is not to say that organisations should never take the Bank of America course, only that serious thought should be given to the decision, whichever way it goes.

To the uninitiated, it is difficult to understand why Quality Circles were adopted in an organisation where there appear to be adequate quality control measures, where management work well together with their staff and the staff themselves appear content in their jobs.

So, if it isn't broken, why try to fix it? The channel for new ideas or ways to make things work better has always existed in the Bank of America. Staff had no real problem in talking to management. And management listened. Some ideas put forward to management were immediately translatable into action, where investigative research was minimal, the advantages were obvious and the disadvantages did not cause too much trouble. Thus the supervisor or manager to whom the problem and solution were proposed could cope with looking at it and having it implemented as part of his job.

When, however, the problem and solution needed more than that, resources became stretched. The more innovative the idea, the more research is needed. The employee producing the suggestion is usually unaware of the full ramifications of his solution, or is too enthusiastic and carried away with the envisaged success of his idea for him to assess the pros and cons objectively. Consider the dilemma of the supervisor to whom the idea is proposed – he can see that he cannot in turn rush to his manager for approval of the new change without a certain amount of research into cost justification, historical data and projected savings. To ask the employee to investigate both the problem and the solution is often not feasible and sometimes unfair. It is often difficult for the employee to see the problem in relation to the rest of his department, let alone the whole bank. Without knowing how to go about it, and probably with very few analytical skills, the employee will soon be discouraged, especially when encountering, as he will, opposition from some of those who will be affected by his solution.

So the problem will tend to be left in the lap of the supervisor to try, as best he can, to do what is necessary to assess it. With the best will in the world, the supervisor will often have to concede to the pressures and priorities of his own job. Lack of time and other problems will take over, and so it is that we hear the all too familiar cries of 'nothing ever happens' and 'I told them, but they didn't do anything about it.'

Senior management in the Bank of America take pains to maximise staff involvement, and an employee suggestion scheme was introduced some years ago to help towards this goal. The scheme is extremely successful both for the bank and the employee, inasmuch as the suggestions made by staff very often carry cost savings of substantial proportions. The employees' financial rewards are based on these savings and the scheme relies largely on this incentive, although ideas based on intangible results such as higher morale or better staff co-operation are also assessed and rewarded in a similar fashion.

How Quality Circles fit into the Bank of America

Quality Circles were already working well in other organisations in the United States when senior management in the bank decided to take a closer look at it. The concept of Quality Circles fitted neatly into bank's philosophy: BankAmericans are respected for what they do and how well they do it, irrespective of their title. In an environment where senior management, through the need to work globally, are evolving as generalists, staff are increasingly becoming the acknowledged specialists in their jobs. However much management would like to be au fait with every facet of a job, it is manifestly not possible. A vehicle to transmit on-the-job difficulties and innovations effectively to management is therefore essential, however trivial the problem may appear to be. Quality Circles provide this means. It gives people already comfortable with their management more than just a communication link; it brings with it the tools for the staff to research and logically follow a problem through to its solution. Because of the clear guidelines for Circles, both sides know where they stand: management won't foist unmanageable problems on the Circles and the Circle members know when selecting their problems that they are not going to try and solve management's problems, but rather everybody works towards building a symbiotic relationship.

Thus Quality Circles run as part of the overall, and long-term, quality programme of the Bank of America.

The story so far

In early 1980, extensive groundwork was done with a consultant who had been responsible for the successful installation of Quality Circles in Lockheed and now ran a consultancy firm specialising in implementing Quality Circles. A training policy was established: all co-ordinators, facilitators and leaders would be trained by the bank's in-house consultants. In the same way, middle management would receive an overview of the concept, with emphasis on their commitment to supporting Circles in their department. A pilot programme was introduced in the World Banking Division in the latter part of 1980. By March 1981, when the first of the ten experimental circles made presentations to their management, it was clear that the programme, even in these early pioneering stages, was a success in every way. Quality Circles were offered throughout the bank. Growth of the Circles is deliberately slow, again according to the guidelines and because the voluntary aspect of the programme is always respected. In May 1983, there were 110 active Circles in three of the four geographic divisions of Bank of America, with an envisaged total of 210 by the end of that year.

There are approximately twenty-two full-time facilitators in the bank and nine Quality of Service Officers who co-ordinate 85 to 100 part-time facilitators.

Support

Training is an essential part of a successful QC programme, but it does not stop after the initial facilitator and leader courses. Regular facilitator workshops are held to ensure an interchange of information and to share experiences. For those Circles who are now sufficiently au fait with the techniques, an advanced training course gives a wider scope and a bigger challenge in their problem solving.

A Quality Circle newsletter is published monthly giving updates on Circle activities throughout the bank and is distributed via the Circles to all employees.

Incentives

Most people feel the need for approbation, and the Circle members are no exception. Whilst the Circles receive support from their managers and encouragement through the sincere interest shown by management in their projects, it was decided by senior management to make an overall excellence award where all Circles may compete. The Circles are encouraged to videotape and submit their management presentations to an evaluating committee in San Francisco. The panel takes into consideration the presentation itself (for example, did all the members in the Circle participate?) and the Circle's appropriate and effective use of the problem-solving techniques. Cost benefits and intangible benefits are also evaluated. Recently Samuel H. Armacost, President of BankAmerica Corporation, honoured the three winning Quality Circles for 1982 at the first annual Quality Circle Awards banquet held in recognition of the Circles' achievements.

Quality Circles run in harmony with the incentive programme previously mentioned, and should a Circle wish to submit their solution to the Ideas in Action programme, as it is called, they may do so as a team and share the reward likewise.

Handing over the maximum reward available under the Ideas in Action of $50,000 to one of the QC Award winning teams, Sam Armacost stressed that, although the savings achieved by the Circle mattered, the other, less tangible benefits were of equal importance. This point is illustrated in that the Circle winning the $50,000 reward through their $700,000 cost saving solution was the runner-up to the award-winning team, which saved the bank a relatively modest sum of $18,480 with their solution.

Case study: London

When the bank offered the programme to its four geographic divisions, the Europe, Middle East and Africa division, headquartered in London, decided to pilot the scheme in their London branch. Once their commitment was made, the search for a facilitator was on. The branch has some 558 employees, and it was obvious that, if the scheme was to be successfully administered, a full-time facilitator was the only answer. Whilst many senior personnel displayed most of the qualities needed for a good facilitator (good organisational skills, ability to talk to senior management, plus all-round experience in the branch's operational units), these people tended to be too far removed from the staff to be readily accepted inside a Circle. It was feared that the Circle members might never really forget the status of such a facilitator and therefore feel uncomfortable at best, and spied upon at worst.

In deciding to adopt Quality Circles, the branch management was determined to adhere to the guidelines, and for good reason: once before a unit in the branch had tried to start something akin to a Circle, which worked well until the initial enthusiasm waned. It was clear that without adherence to the guidelines, meetings thus started cannot claim to be Quality Circles, nor can they succeed in their aims.

In March of 1982 the Head of Operations heard of another failure – someone only vaguely familiar with the guidelines of Quality Circles had tried it, believing that sincerity and enthusiasm will overcome the other obstacles. The first meeting ended in enough discord for that person to realise the facts as they apply to a real Quality Circle, and the idea was abandoned. Working on the basis that first failures are the seeds of experience, an approach was made to this person and the branch had its first facilitator.

Leadership training

The facilitator's training, conducted in San Francisco, included first-hand experience by sitting in on some of the Quality Circle meetings there. Leader training was also provided, since the facilitator would be expected to take over from an absent leader at short notice.

Back in London, the facilitator and co-ordinator organised a day-long seminar for the branch's department heads. The overview included the goals of Quality Circles and their guidelines. Great care was taken that enthusiasm for the new project did not overshadow the commitment asked for, not just in terms of the manager's personal support, but in the employees' time that will be needed for attendance of a Circle. Those managers who decided after the seminar to proceed with Quality Circles in their departments worked with the facilitator in identifying the most likely candidates for leaders. These people, although mostly supervisors, also included senior clerks who, their managers felt, could benefit from the leader training even if they decided not to become a Quality Circle leader.

A brief presentation to the leaders resulted in a number of volunteers for the first leader training session in November 1982. The co-ordinator conducted the session, which lasted three days and covered the basic problem-solving techniques used by Quality Circles. Consensus decision making was another area that received attention and the leaders were also instructed in how to run effective meetings. At the end of their third day, the recruits all volunteered to lead a Circle, and by the end of December the branch had six Circles well on their way in learning their new skills.

Setting up the Circles
Until the first leaders were trained, Quality Circles had not been advertised in the branch. The thought behind this was that until management were comfortable with the concept and there was a clear indication where Circles could be started with full support from the manager, there was no point in getting staff members interested in areas where Circles were either never due to start or where the manager had adopted a wait-and-see approach.

When the new leaders were ready to recruit members for their Circles, a memorandum from the head of the London Branch went to each employee, together with an information sheet on Quality Circles. The memo explained the purpose of Quality Circles and why the branch had decided to adopt the programme. Employees were invited to contact the facilitator for information about the implementation plan.

The facilitator co-ordinated the employee-orientation sessions, coaching the manager and new leader in their roles for the hour-long meeting. All employees normally reporting to the supervisor-cum-leader were asked by the manager to attend the session. The manager, after pledging his support for the Circles, left the meeting to the leader and facilitator to initiate the recruits further in the concept of Circles. The training programme used by the bank provides a videotape for each technique as well as an introductory tape. This tape is played at the orientation and the employees are given an opportunity to put questions to the leader and facilitator. As with the leader recruits, the voluntary aspect of joining a circle is stressed by all presenters. The employees are given three days to make up their minds.

Subsequent recruitment of employees was linked to two more leader training sessions. Where the first leader training provided as many leaders as recruits, the second and third session produced a more cautious breed. Now that the new recruits had a reference point in the first leaders, 80 per cent acceptance was the norm, and showed a realistic assessment of what is asked for in terms of personal commitment from a leader. The opposite appeared true for new Circle members – the feedback they received from 'veteran' members invariably resulted in their being persuaded of the benefits that Circles would bring to them personally, their jobs and future.

At the end of June 1983, 13 Circles were active in the London branch – demand for Circles had not yet peaked, and a further training course for potential leaders had to be held in the autumn.

Success stories

Problems that Circles have tackled include inadequate handling of telephone messages, where the Circle members decided that the main cause of their problem lay with themselves; thus their solution took the form of a mission statement pledging proper routing of calls, and taking meaningful messages. Another group has dealt with the redrafting of computer input forms – an unexpected spin-off was the appreciation felt by the input clerks for the Circle having sought their opinion before the final introduction of the new form. Tidying up a department has led another Circle into all kinds of ramifications of what appeared to be a relatively straight-forward problem. Their many recommendations include circulation of bank publications which used to remain undistributed and therefore unread, and improved work-flow from reorganisation of furniture. The installation of a staff-monitored system for a photocopier now ensures shared responsibility for its maintenance, and contin-uous training by the Circle members in its operation has cut down on wastage.

Circles also invariably get a range of smaller problems sorted out, often things that have been frustrating people for ages, and perhaps more important, a range of intan-gible improvements begin to be seen quite early in the programme. One such example is that employees talk to each other more openly about their jobs, and spend time trying to understand each other's roles. Members become more introspective, and less anxious to lay the blame on others.

With the exception of a few Circles whose problem selection tended towards making their lives at the office more luxurious rather than more efficient, Circle members show a remarkable degree of self-examination. Most members are ruthless in identifying causes where they are the main wrongdoers.

Another aspect of this is the development of higher levels of understanding of the work of other depart-ments. By the very nature of their jobs, employees are sometimes isolated from the rest of the bank's functions. When looking at problems, however, they are often given an insight into how other departments function and the reasons for a particular procedure have only become clear to them by virtue of their own investigation into both sides of a problem.

Again an intangible, but vital benefit of the approach is the team-building philosophy of Quality Circles. This is best illustrated by the following example: Part of a solution identified by the whole Circle had previously been submitted by one of the Circle members to the bank's incentive scheme. This scheme carries a reward based on the total cost savings generated by the idea. The member decided to withdraw his solution, so that the whole Circle could share the reward if that part of the solution is finally submitted to the Ideas in Action programme by the group. This gesture means that the Circle member will have to share what could have been a substantial reward with the rest of the team – his share will be a sixth.

Circles certainly develop skills and abilities. By the same token, especially where the leader is concerned, weaknesses which did not show clearly in the supervisor's normal role are sometimes highlighted in his Circle leadership. Part of the facilitator's job is to ensure that the supervisor is given all the sympathetic support and understanding necessary to help overcome individual difficulties, and also to develop his confidence and ability in the role of both Circle leader and supervisor. It is this opportunity which makes Quality Circles such a powerful method of developing supervisory skills.

It is too soon for the London Branch of the bank to claim all the benefits that Circles undoubtedly bring to an organisation. Suffice it to say that the management's respect for the Circles and the greater understanding already created so early in the programme between departments and employees are proof enough that Quality Circles will continue alongside the bank's overall quality management programme towards maintaining excellence of service.

Keeping going I: Wedgwood*

Dick Fletcher

The Wedgwood case is based on an address given by Dick Fletcher to an IPA conference on 'The Quest for Quality of Working Life'. Dick Fletcher was then asked to add a short update to this article, which he has done.

The points from the Wedgwood story which cry out for attention are, firstly, the importance and effect of total top management commitment, and secondly, the effect that a charismatic, skilful and committed facilitator can have on a programme.

A vital point about the commitment of top management is that, if it is not visible and believable, it may as well not be there. There are programmes where senior people are genuinely committed and yet they find it extremely difficult to communicate the depth of their belief to the workforce. As with all life, it is people's own perceptions that determine how they respond. If staff do not believe that their boss is committed, that is the reality the boss has to live with. Top management at Wedgwood have been able to state their commitment clearly and in a way that is tangible and credible and the result is clear to see.

The role of the facilitator in Quality Circles is a vital and central one. There are no absolute rules as to the part of the business he should come from or indeed his characteristics as an individual. Successful facilitators have worked in every type of department from Quality Control to Production, from Engineering to Accounts, and had all sorts of personalities and interests. It is clear, however, that the better the facilitator the more successful will be

---

* Part of this chapter is based on an article that first appeared in the Summer 1982 volume of *Industrial Participation* and is reproduced here with their kind permission.

the programme, and that good facilitators do seem to have some things in common. One, they are genuine enthusiasts about the approach, whose enthusiasm 'bubbles over' and transmits itself to others. Two, they tend not to be cynical people, not only in relation to Quality Circles but to life in general and their organisation specifically. In other words they tend to see the glass as half full rather than half empty. Three, they have the ability to communicate clearly and accurately to people at many different levels of the company and to see things from other people's point of view. Four, they usually have a well-developed capacity for enjoying the work and helping others to enjoy it as well. Having fun is a central part of successful Quality Circles programmes.

One organisation with a large and successful Quality Circles programme, asked how they select their facilitators, replied that they wait until there is snow on the ground, then they organise a big party for everyone, and when people are leaving they look for the person who doesn't leave any footprints! As is the case in any walk of life, there are some people who intuitively do the job well, and others who find it more difficult. Given good initial training, sufficient back-up development and at least an element of the characteristics outlined above, most people will be able to do the job successfully.

About two years ago we were in the state that I think many companies are in today: we had heard something about Quality Circles, and were wondering whether it would help us to introduce them at Wedgwood, but we had not decided one way or the other. So what I want to do is to describe why and how we did so, and the enjoyment and the benefits all the participants have since derived from them. Why did we eventually decide to go ahead? The reason, the real reason, was the survival of our company. About three years ago the company had about 8,000 employees; now that has gone down to under 5,000. They are divided among 12 factories, all within a five-mile radius. Now those may not sound very large numbers compared with some firms, but we felt that with what for us seemed a quite large factory, the senior management was losing touch with shopfloor operatives and also with middle management and supervision. So the person who started us on the road to Quality Circles was the man at the very top – the Chairman of the company.

I believe the fact that Quality Circles have been successful at Wedgwood – and they have been remarkably successful – is basically for one reason and one reason only: that there has been absolute and total commitment from the very beginning, from the top and right down to the bottom. And that, I believe, is absolutely essential for any company that is considering Quality Circles – total commitment. If you start off at half-cock, your Circles will go off at half-cock, and one failing Circle can do more damage than twenty good ones can achieve.

The decision to start

It was early in 1980 that we first heard about Quality Circles from an article in a magazine. To find out more, we sent some of our training officers to a Quality Circle seminar. They came back and said they really wanted to see some Quality Circles in action, so they arranged to visit another firm nearby, where Circles had been established. They were very impressed with what they saw, and asked who had trained them. It was a consultant. So we invited the same consultant to come to Wedgwood to make a presentation to the Board, which he did in October 1980, and subsequently he was asked to introduce Circles in our company.

Why did the Board decide to go ahead? As I have already mentioned, there was the feeling that senior management was losing touch with the shopfloor. In much of British industry we are stuck with a 'we and they' attitude that somehow has to be stopped. Quality Circles is one way of getting round it because, for the first time ever, Quality Circles enable the people who are doing a regular job in the factory – such as, in our case, making plates or decorating cups – to play a very important part in the running of the factory, and to know that they are doing so. It is, after all, the people who have spent much of their lives sticking handles on cups who know more about that job, and its problems and possibilities for improvement, than anyone else, often even than their managers. Managers, certainly in our industry, are basically administrators, and we tend to change them around from one job to another, so that often they have no real practical knowledge of the jobs their people are actually doing – which are often very tricky jobs requiring a great deal of skill and practice.

So through Quality Circles we believed that we might find out from the people who are actually doing the job what are the problems associated with it, and how they can be solved – and this has proved to be the case: we are now getting answers to many of the problems that we had never been able to solve before.

How we began
That was why we decided to introduce Quality Circles. After the original presentation to the Board, and the decision to go ahead, the first 'facilitator' was chosen – I was he. 'Facilitator' sounds an extraordinary word, possibly one should say 'co-ordinator'. The next step was for the consultant to make a seven-hour presentation to senior management, because you have to have senior management on your side right from the start. This was to explain exactly what Circles are and what they could do. Then he made four-hour presentations to middle management and to the trade unions – note that, the trade unions, that is most important. These were actually split into five half-days, so as to cover everyone in relatively small groups, each having four hours with him in all.

Then I as the facilitator had to undergo one complete day's training, which was extremely interesting.

Choosing and training the first Circle leaders

We then chose our first twelve Circle leaders. We chose particular people who were chargehands or foremen or forewomen in areas where we thought 'the grass was greenest' – in the 'non-aggro' areas, perhaps I should say, where we thought it would be easiest to introduce Circles. I think this is a very important point. If you are going to introduce Quality Circles, you should try to ensure that the first ones are going to be successful, so as to get off to a good start. Don't start in the more difficult areas, even though those may be the ones with the biggest problems!

We did not push or 'con' these first twelve leaders into it. We said: 'We think you are the sort of person who could do this and would enjoy it.' The consultant then gave those first 12 Circle leaders twenty-two hours' training – three days. So we had twelve trained leaders, ready to start up twelve Quality Circles. But we decided to start with six first circles, then add another six a month later.

Voluntary participation

We wanted each Circle to have eight to ten members, who were to be entirely voluntary. So the Circle leaders went around the members of their workgroup saying something like: 'Look, Mary, I think you are the sort of person who might enjoy this.' And the response might be: 'Well, I'll come if Bill and his wife will come too', and so on. But it was made absolutely clear to everyone that it was entirely voluntary; if they came and didn't like it, they could leave at any time; or they could even leave half-way through a project and come back three months later.

So we got the nucleus of the first six Circles, and we started to train them as to what it was all about, with me sitting in the whole time. And then the second six Circles on the same basis. All the time we emphasised not only that it was voluntary, but that it was a thing to enjoy. It shouldn't be looked upon as hard work. It is enjoyment. And it is of interest that, of all Circles we started with, the original members are all still with us – so they are still enjoying it.

The development of Quality Circles

Extending the programme

Then we did a repeat of the whole thing, choosing another twelve leaders, training them, and getting two more successive groups of six Circles started. In this way the programme has snowballed through the company to over 100 Circles – a large number for this country but quite insignificant compared with America and Japan.

What has made it possible is that we now have so many full-time facilitators – seven in all. If each facilitator starts up just two new Circles a week, that is 14 in all. So we now have 104 Circles, with 807 members, plus 130 trained leaders, out of a total workforce of about 4,000. So far the Circles are all factory-based – we have not as yet involved our office or support staff but we are about to do so.

There are now Circles in ten out of our twelve factories, and we have seven factory steering committees – these are a group of people in each factory who control the basic principles of the Circles to make sure they are going along the right lines. They meet about once every two or three months with their facilitators.

Circle presentations to senior management

Once the Circles have chosen their own problems that they want to tackle, and have analysed the causes, they come up with a solution and make their presentation to senior management – this is a very important part of the programme. The presentation may be made to the Company Chairman if the Circle thinks it is important enough; many presentations are made to other Board members or General Managers. So far there have been 297 such individual presentations. The average time between presentations – ie the time it takes a Circle to identify, analyse and solve a problem – is five weeks. Some have been as short as three weeks, but one case took as long as nine months. That was a problem that involved a lot of hard work and a great deal of data gathering.

Cost and returns

The cost per year to run a Circle is £1,000. That may sound a lot of money, and the company accounts department may want to know where it all goes and whether it is worth it. Most of it pays the wages of the full-time facilitators, who are all fairly senior, and the wages of all the Circle members for the time they spend in Circle meetings – we charge all that in. It also covers the cost of training. We do not, however, charge in overheads for space used and so on.

The return, at the present time, is at least three to one – that is a figure that we can actually prove if any accountant challenges it. I think in reality it is nearer four or five to one. Some companies, such as Rolls Royce, claim a ten to one return; in Japan, they claim the average is about 30:1. But quite frankly I do not think this is the most important factor. It is the spin-off in people's enthusiasm and in the difference in attitudes that Circles have generated which is a much more important benefit.

Circles choose their own names

The members of each Circle are of course all people working in the same general area and doing the same or similar jobs – basically members in the same workgroup. Usually they choose a name for their Circle, which in most cases has some relation to their work. Choosing a name is in fact one of the first tasks we give them when training a new Circle in brainstorming – and some come up with quite extraordinary names! One of the earliest Circles is called 'Quest', which stands for 'Quality Unites Enamellers and Staff Together'. 'Trigger Flickers' are the people who spray the glaze on; 'Whirlers' are those who fill the moulds, because they always have to do this while the moulds are rotating; the fitters called their Circle 'Ubendem Wemendem'.

Domestic illustration of how Circles work

All our Circles at Wedgwood are obviously involved in operations related to the manufacture of pottery, so to appreciate how they choose, tackle and solve problems one needs to know something of the technical processes involved. But to demonstrate in more general and homely terms just how a Circle would tackle a problem that everyone can identify with, consider a non-factory situation. Imagine an ordinary home, a house run by Mother with some seven or eight other members of the family (to make it about the size of a typical Quality Circle).

The first stage of training is to sit round in a brainstorming session. The leader of the house, not Mother, says: 'Now what are the problems in and around this house – what things are wrong with it?' One member of the family says, 'The fire goes out too often.' So they write that down – in a Quality Circle we would use a flipchart. Another says, 'Everything in the house has dog hairs all over it.' Another, 'The windows won't close properly.' 'Toast is always getting burnt.' 'All the cutlery is stained.' 'The water isn't hot enough.' 'The house faces the wrong way.' 'There's too much traffic on the road.' 'You can't hear the doorbell.' And so on. They keep at it until no one has any further suggestions.

Which problems can we solve ourselves?

Then they go through all these things one by one, in a process which in our Circles we call 'evaluation', and they draw a circle around all the things that the Circle members, or the people of the household, could solve themselves – or think they could.

- Fire keeps going out
- Dog hairs everywhere
- Burnt toast
- Stained cutlery
- Water not hot enough

When it comes to the windows that won't close, they say that it is probably a professional's job, so they put a star against it – get in outside help (or, in a factory, possibly 'ask the so-and-so Circle if they can solve it'). Similarly with the doorbell, unless one of the family is a trained electrician.

'House faces the wrong way.' Well, there is nothing anyone can do about that, so cross it out altogether. Similarly with too much traffic in the road.

So the family is left to see (in this very simplified version) which of five problems can be solved immediately without any further fuss. 'Stained cutlery' – simply purchase some Silver Dip and Johnny offers to clean it. 'Water not hot enough' – turn up the thermostat.

Deciding which problem to tackle first

Now they are left with three rather more intractable problems, and they cast votes as to which they think are the most pressing ones to get down to first of all – not on a 'one man one vote' system, they can vote for as many as they like – simply the ones they think are worth tackling sooner rather than later. Nor does it mean they are dodging the others, just that they will come back to them later. It turns out that three members think the dog hairs are important enough, four the fire going out, and all eight the problem of the burnt toast. This is marked on the brainstorm list, as shown on p. 100. (In a factory Circle there would probably be many more than three problems left, and a greater spread of voting.)

Although in this simple family situation it is clear enough what is the first problem to be tackled, in a factory Circle they would go on to draw a Pareto Chart –

what words we use! – really just a bar chart, as shown below, a simple way of showing which problems Circle members think are the most important ones, and in what order.

Having chosen 'Burnt Toast' as the most important problem, they then have to prove to Mother that they are right. One of the worst mistakes that Circles can make is to produce what are really no more than opinions, so that when they come to make their presentation to management, all they can say is 'We think it is so and so.' Management's response will be, 'We don't want to know

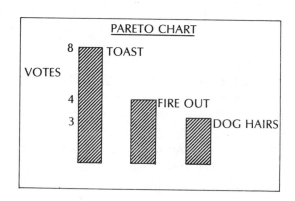

what you think, we want facts – only if you can really show what is wrong can we go along with you.'

Collecting data

So the Circle makes out a data sheet, as shown, and they work out, in this case over a period of three weeks to show that it is not just coincidence, on which days the toast gets burnt most.

DATA GATHERING		
NUMBER OF PIECES OF TOAST BURNT		
M	1 1 1 1 1 1	6
T	1 1 1 1 1 1 1 1 1	9
W		0
T	1 1 1	3
F	1 1 1 1	4
S		0
S	1 1 1 1 1	5
M	1 1 1 1 1 1 1 1 1 1	10
T	1 1 1 1 1 1 1 1 1 1 1 1 1	13
W		0
T	1	1
F	1 1 1	3
S		0
S	1 1 1 1 1 1	6
M	1 1 1 1 1 1 1 1 1	9
T	1 1 1 1 1 1 1 1 1 1 1 1 1 1	14
W		0
T	1 1	2
F	1 1 1 1	4
S		0
S	1 1 1 1 1	5

Clearly it varies from day to day. Mondays are pretty poor days, Tuesdays are terrible, on Wednesdays there is no problem, and on Thursdays and Fridays it is not so bad as on Mondays and Tuesdays. Saturdays, like Wednesdays, are all right, obviously because they get fresh bread then. On Sundays the problem starts to build up, and so back to the bad Mondays and Tuesdays.

It has therefore been shown that there really is a

problem, and also that the problem has variants – in this case, some days that are much worse than others. Then, to follow our standard Quality Circle procedure, a simple 'histogram' like the one shown here would be prepared as a quick way of showing on which days the toast gets more burnt than on others.

HISTOGRAM NUMBER OF PIECES OF TOAST BURNT OVER THREE WEEKS							
	M	T	W	T	F	S	S
WEEK 1.	6	9	0	3	4	0	5
2.	10	13	0	1	3	0	6
3.	9	14	0	2	4	0	5
TOTAL	25	36	0	6	11	0	16

Cause and effect

Now we come to the most important thing in the whole of Quality Circle work. We prepare what is called a 'Cause and Effect' diagram (see opposite), or, as it is sometimes called, an 'Ishikawa' diagram after Dr Ishikawa of Japan, or, because of its skeletal shape, a 'fishbone' diagram. First, on the right-hand-side, we state the problem: 'Toast gets burnt in toaster.' Then we try to think of all the different things that might cause or contribute to the problem, putting them down in various related categories. We do it by going round and round the group, asking each member in turn, one at a time, to make one suggestion. If anyone has no suggestion, or no further suggestion, he says 'pass'. That does not carry any criticism of him. Nor is there any criticism of any of the suggestions that may be made – that would simply put people off.

Eventually, when no one has any further suggestions – everyone passes – the leader goes round the group again to ask which of the problems people think are important, and puts rings around them, giving a completed cause and effect diagram.

Cause and effect diagram

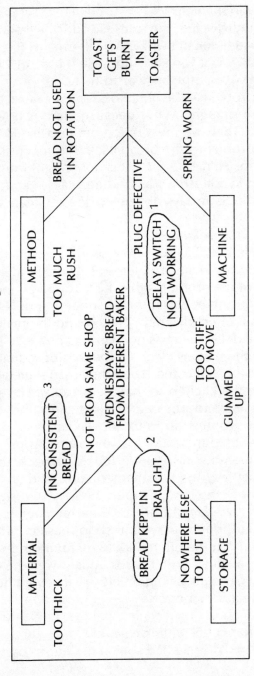

Finding the solutions

Then they discuss the causes, and the solutions. The delay switch doesn't work. Why doesn't it? It is too stiff to move. Why is it too stiff? Because it has got clogged up. Right, we know the answer to that one.

Next problem – the bread dries out because it is kept in the open draught. Why? Because there is nowhere else to put it. Then we must find a better place to keep it.

Next problem – the bread itself. It is inconsistent. Why is it inconsistent? Because it is not bought from the same shop on Wednesdays as on Saturdays – and the bread bought on Saturdays obviously doesn't keep so well.

Implementing solutions

The Circle now has some very good answers to what are obviously the main problems. They have identified the priority of the problems they have to solve – indicated by putting numbers against the ringed problems in the cause and effect diagram. They found the real key problem – the delay switch is not working properly. So, first of all, they thoroughly clean up the toaster so that the delay switch can be adjusted. Then they rearrange what is kept where in the kitchen so that the bread can be stored in a better place and not in a draught. And they organise a change of routine so as to get similar bread throughout the week by purchasing it at the same shop.

One member also undertook to check the correct toaster setting, and put an instruction card on the side to show where the switch should be set for fresh, one-day-old, and two-day-old bread. One member had noticed that bread bought from one shop toasted more quickly than that from the other and, as he found from the Circle that they all liked both breads equally well, he calculated that a 25 per cent saving on electricity could be made by using bread number one.

Demonstrating the improvement

So this family Circle had solved the burnt toast problem,

and as a spin-off had made a financial saving as well. To prove that they had solved the problem, in a factory situation they would prepare another graph to show the difference – how infrequently the toast was now burnt, compared with before. This control chart would be the basis of their presentation to management.

IMPROVEMENT ACHIEVED – CONTROL CHART NUMBER OF PIECES OF TOAST BURNT		
M	1 1	2
T	1 1	2
W		0
T	1	1
F	1 1	2
S		0
S	1	1
M	1	1
T		0
W	1 1	2
T	1 1	2
F	1 1 1	3
S		0
S	1	1
M	1 1	2
T	1 1	2
W		0
T	1	1
F	1	1
S		0
S	1 1	2

It also provides a check to ensure that the improvement is maintained. This is important in Circle work. There can be a wonderful blaze of glory when the presentation is made, but if after six weeks things have fallen back to the same state as before nothing really will have been achieved. It is important therefore to have some means of checking to see that things continue to be kept up to the proper standard.

Problems solved by Circles at Wedgwood

Now to convert that picture of a Quality Circle into our factories at Wedgwood, to show the kinds of problem that have been solved, but without going into technical details that probably only other pottery people could follow.

Avoiding wastage

One problem that has been common to the whole pottery industry throughout its history is that, when you make top-quality bone china plates, you can only make 40 plates from each mould, and you have always had to throw the first three away because they were no good. Nobody had ever come up with a solution. But the mould makers' Quality Circle in one of our factories decided to tackle this problem, and came up with something absolutely novel, that no one had ever thought of before – and now we don't throw those first three plates away any more, nor do any of the other factories in our Wedgwood group – and of course it didn't take long before it got to our competitors as well, but I am quite pleased about that, because it all helps the industry as a whole, and we are a very close-knit community. But this is just one of the things that would never have happened if the people who have actually been making the moulds all their lives had not got together and put their minds to the problem.

Eliminating spoilt plates

Another problem tackled by one of our earliest Circles was the identification marks on the back of plates. It is perhaps rather strange that every hand-painted plate has an identification mark on its back to show who painted it. Now these marks, which were chosen by each individual for herself, vary greatly in complexity and therefore in the time it took to make them, but they also had a nasty habit of sometimes partly flaking off or falling off during firing, and therefore ruining the plate below. The Circle came up with this solution: a simple dot rather than a complicated mark, with the positioning of the dot in relation to the backstamp as the individual identifying device.

The same Circle then tackled another problem – the elimination of colour specks and 'crawl' that ruined so many plates, the cause of which had been absolutely unknown previously. With some of the larger plates that sell at £100 or so each, the saving here was quite extraordinary.

Another Circle designed a new trolley for moving the unfired pottery to the kiln that greatly reduced the risk of pieces of pottery knocking together and being broken.

Working with manufacturers to improve quality of materials
Another designed a quite different and much more effectively-shaped brush for painting plates. This they did in co-operation with the brush manufacturer, by going to visit his factory in London and explaining their problems with the traditional type of brush. This was a wonderful experience both for the manufacturer and for our Circle members – the people who actually used the product discussing their real problems and needs with the people who made it. As a result of this experience, most of our suppliers now have to work with the Circles that use their materials – and there is no better judge of the quality of materials coming into a factory than the people who have actually got to use them!

One Circle has tackled the question of the factory bus service, and the loading and unloading points – and, in conjunction with the bus company, significantly improved the service and facilities for the very many of our employees who depend on it to get to and from work.

Strengths and weaknesses

What are the pitfalls?

With over 100 Circles now operating I could give innumerable examples of Quality Circle achievements. But perhaps I should mention also what the pitfalls are, because it is important to know what these may be, in order to steer clear of them. In fact, we have not had any really serious problems. We have had some people dropping out of a Circle because someone else is in it, or perhaps because they have not agreed with the solution the Circle put forward. Often it only needs the facilitator to keep his ear to the ground and know what is going on to smooth out that sort of difficulty before it gets serious.

I think the only genuine trouble we have had is that some of our junior managers have tended to feel pilloried when they have taken on the role of Circle leader. This we have found particularly with some of the older people, who are perhaps not quite as good as they like to think they are; and in many cases they have been superseded by up-and-coming operatives who have shown remarkable signs of being just the right people to run the Circle. This has undoubtedly caused a certain amount of resentment.

But the really good people among our junior managers and supervisors have derived great benefit from the Circles, and the improvement in personal relations, and the fact that people now feel very much a part of the factory, are very encouraging.

Improvements from Circles at Wedgwood

Wedgwood is not just a factory full of people painting flowers on the sides of cups. It is a very tightly-controlled factory – which is why it is so successful. Even in the days when we were having so many cutbacks, our turnover and profit figures were maintained.

The introduction of Quality Circles has been accepted as one of the main reasons why our quality and our productivity have improved. In addition our industrial relations have improved out of all measure – because people now once again, even though we have grown so big, feel they are back in a smaller unit where they can speak directly to people they couldn't speak to before. Quality Circles have certainly done something for all our Circle members at Wedgwood that otherwise I believe could never have happened.

Commitment at the top

But, as I said at the beginning, if you want to start Quality Circles you really do have to convince people right at the top, and get their full commitment. And let me end by giving one example of this commitment at Wedgwood that demonstrates the extraordinary support from the Chairman downwards that makes my life so very easy.

Now Wedgwood is a very tight firm, a very keen firm, and trading is difficult. No money is spent on travelling other than travelling for sales. However, last year I went to the Chairman, and said I would like to go to the international meeting in Tokyo on Quality Circles. His immediate response was that of course I must go. Then he asked, 'Who is your best Circle leader?' That was a difficult question to answer. We had 22 Circles at that time, and there were five leaders whom I regarded as all equally good. So he said, 'Put those five names in a hat and I will pick one out' – which he did. 'And this one will go to Tokyo with you.'

And for a Circle leader who, as it happened had only been married three weeks earlier, and had never been further than Folkestone in his life, it was a remarkable experience – it has really made him. A year later, another Circle leader, who again was one of the five best and whose name was picked out of the hat, went to that year's international Quality Circle meeting in Tokyo with my second facilitator. Now that is what I call total commitment from the top.

An update

Quality Circles started at Wedgwood late in 1980. Now in 1983 we have some 150 circles looked after by 8 full-time facilitators. Sixty per cent of the leaders are operatives, the remaining 40 per cent are first-line management.

Circles meet for one hour each week at a fixed time. The Circle leader often spends extra time before and after meetings discussing progress with the facilitators.

The facilitator sits in at meetings if required. He is needed particularly in the later stages building up to a presentation. He is entirely responsible for implementing the outcome of the presentation once it has been sanctioned by management.

Leaders are given as much support as is possible. Extra instruction courses are held for them in small groups and occasionally well-known speakers are invited to address an assembly of all leaders at once.

Advanced leader training is given to groups of leaders twice a year, away from the factory and in conjunction with leaders from other firms who are actively running Quality Circles. Each year a facilitator and one leader go to an International Convention and factory tour in Japan. Wedgwood also plays host to the bi-annual Japanese Quality Circle tours, when their Circles and Wedgwood Circles make a series of presentations to one another.

Co-operation

Wedgwood Circles tackle all sorts of project in their area: Productivity, Quality, Reduction of Scrap, Quality of Life and also Environmental Improvements. They request visits from suppliers in order to ensure that materials and tools are exactly what they want. Circles visit manufacturers' factories to see articles being made so that they can discuss at first hand exactly what they want. If the manufacturer happens to have adopted the Quality Circle approach to working life then so much the better because immediately there is common ground.

Quality Circles often combine together to solve joint

or related problems, not forgetting also that each department in production is the immediate customer of the one before. Circles are therefore encouraged to make or repeat presentations to the other members of their department or associated departments. Circles are also in constant demand to make presentations at Works Council Meetings and have also presented to visiting dignitaries, Members of Parliament and County Council Chairmen.

Circles usually choose their own problems. Occasionally management suggests a problem, and Circles usually welcome this since they know that they, the Circle, have the final say as to whether they tackle it or not.

Presentations

Presentations to management take place on an average once every twelve weeks. At these presentations all the working papers are displayed from the original brainstorm through Pareto Analysis to Cause and Effect Classification and Analysis. Data Sheets are displayed showing the results of Data Gathering and on occasions Pie Charts, Histograms and Defect Location Charts back up the project. Quality Circles know only too well that it is facts and not opinions which win the day. Good presentations of solutions to senior management are the outward visible sign of a good Circle project.

At a presentation it may be the first time that a Circle member has come face to face with the company production director or managing director; both soon realise just how much each has to offer the other for the common good of the factory and themselves.

The projects

These fall into four main groups:

1   Quality improvements
2   Productivity improvements
3   Improvements to the quality of working life
4   Environmental improvements

and the 'spin-offs' from these groups are:

1   Much more involvement at all levels
2   Greater understanding of each other's viewpoints and problems
3   Improved communication upwards and downwards.

From the many, many projects taken on and implemented here at Wedgwood a few are given below to show the wide scope of the subjects:

Easing of access points to grease nipples, dip sticks and oil filling points on machinery.
Lubrication schedule for *all* factory machinery.
Improvements to security of personal possessions in workplace.
Re-layout of workplace.
New method of mould drying.
Controlled method of de-humidifying clayware.
Re-design of casting workbench.
Improved colour storage and dispensing in hand-enamelling department.
Universal support for ware during firing.
New trollies for clay movement.
Improved works' buses arrangements and parking and picking up points on factory.
Improved painting and lining brushes.
Reduction of air pin holes in plaster moulds.
De-clogging of plaster supply line.
Improved lighting at workplace.
Better reclaim of precious metals.
Improved conditioning and storage of clay handles.
Re-design of spray hood and work holders.
Planned maintenance scheme for spray guns.
New box-opening device for packing department.

Conclusions and advice
The concept of Quality Circles will work provided that it

has unstinted support from the top and is not looked upon as a management tool, which it is not. A good facilitator, as senior as possible, is an asset.

It will take time to get it fully installed and this will go through stages of being tolerated through acceptance to being welcomed. It will take many knocks and the root cause of the anti-lobby is nearly always ignorance, so more involvement and education into the concept is an obvious antidote. As to advice:

1   Get a good consultant with a proven track record to start you off.
2   Don't skimp training or short-circuit the basic rules. They are internationally accepted and have been for years. They are simple, sound and sensible – why should you be different?
3   Get everyone involved, the board, management at all levels, unions and suppliers.

Keeping going
II: May and Baker

Dianne Moore and John Drinkwater

The May and Baker case history is particularly interesting because it is one of the longest-running Quality Circles programmes in the UK. It has been through different phases, and for the benefit of organisations that are considering the introduction of Quality Circles it will be worth briefly reviewing the issues that seem to have affected them. The first is that, although it is not mentioned specifically in the case history, the programme had the active backing of the Trade Union executive from the beginning. There is no doubt that this active encouragement was a great stimulus.

The second point worth noting concerns the role of facilitator. May and Baker began with a facilitator who was virtually full-time, and the programme flourished under his guidance, and that of the part-time co-ordinator. Unfortunately after about twelve months the facilitator left the company, and at around the same time the co-ordinator found himself unable to continue putting in the required amount of time. It was fortunate that the company had already concluded that to have one facilitator was 'putting all the eggs in one basket' and that it would be more sensible to have a team of trained facilitators. Volunteers were sought, came forward and were trained. This worked well for a time, but once the co-ordinator was unable to spend time on the programme, it became more difficult for some managers to organise their time to devote the requisite amount to the Quality Circle groups. This leads to a useful rule of thumb: ideally there should be a full-time facilitator to begin with. This will mean, at the very least, that the required amount of time is being put into the programme. If part-time facilitators are used it should be a standard practice that they agree to see at least one group through to maturity and self-sufficiency. In this latter situation the co-ordinator needs to be very active in ensuring that the time is in fact being put in, since it is all too easy for other short-term pressures to come in the way.

Another feature of the May and Baker case history is the very direct relationship there appears to be between success and the active and overt commitment of management. It is a subject often talked about in relation to Quality Circles, and in an organisation of the size of May and Baker there will inevitably be all shades of opinion. It is interesting to note how sensitive members of staff are to the style of their managers, and how they seem to take this into account when forming their view about the Quality Circle approach. Workgroups that perceive their managers as negative will often claim that it is not worth their while forming a group, and even if they do decide to go ahead, they will sometimes do so with a somewhat fatalistic attitude.

The fourth useful lesson concerns the relative importance of tangible benefits within the Quality Circle scheme. The three main aims of the approach are, in order of importance, staff involvement, people development and the generation of tangible benefits. The third, tangible benefits, is important in two respects. Firstly, the Quality Circles themselves are invariably interested in 'keeping score' of their achievements, and this usually implies being interested in achieving tangible benefits of one kind or another. Secondly, it has to be recognised that Quality Circles do cost the organisation a substantial amount of money. One hour a week for members and the additional time of leaders and facilitators does not come free. Most organisations, therefore, will hope for some payback in tangible terms as well as the more intangible benefits of involvement, development, satisfaction and morale. The key, however, is to recognise that tangible benefits really are third in order of importance and that pressure should not be put on groups to work on problems which are likely to yield financial benefits. An aspect of this is that groups which do work on a subject which yields such rewards should not be treated in any way differently from other groups, and neither should groups such as the Bottle Inspection Quality Circle in the case history, which saved a large sum of money, be put on a pedestal for this reason alone. It is much more important

> to reinforce and recognise groups that successfully use the principles and problem-solving practices of the approach, whether or not they save money. This principle was reinforced earlier in the book in the Bank of America case history where, in evaluating entries for their 'Ideas in Action' awards, the judges gave first prize to a group that had used the problem-solving structure expertly with only a small tangible benefit, over a group which had saved much more.

May and Baker is an international organisation which employs approximately 4,000 people in the United Kingdom. Its operations include the manufacture of agro-chemicals, pharmaceuticals, animal health products, industrial chemicals, laboratory chemicals and photographic products.

There are four main locations in the United Kingdom. Firstly, Dagenham, where commercial activities, research and development and production are carried out. In addition there is a large facility for pharmaceutical packaging. Secondly, Norwich has a production site for agro-chemicals, industrial and pharmaceutical chemicals, certain photographic products and additionally pharmaceutical formulation and packaging. Thirdly, the centre of the United Kingdom laboratory chemicals activity is situated at Barton Moss; in addition to the packing and storing of laboratory chemicals for sale in the United Kingdom and overseas, the category sales office is located there. Fourthly, the company has a research station at Ongar.

May and Baker is at the forefront of the industries with which it competes. Its future depends upon the effectiveness, quality, safety, reputation and profitability of its products. It has to operate in and accommodate a rapidly changing environment, in particular the demand for new products, the introduction of new technology and economic and social changes. In other words, it has to be adaptable.

May and Baker considers that this adaptability depends upon its people, and that it must ensure that all employees have the widest opportunity to develop their capabilities at work. Therefore it is company policy that all employees operating in this changing environment have the opportunity to influence how their work is done and how it is developed and improved.

Quality Circles is one of the methods used to enable this policy to be put into action. Quality Circles have helped produce various benefits by utilising the expertise of employees which previously had not been drawn on. Suggestions put forward by Circles have led to a wide range of benefits from cost savings, reduction of wastage and improved working methods. Furthermore, it has been found that being a member of a Circle can bring out individual strengths, leading to a more personal development and increased scope. The company has said that a good organisation is one where there is a good fit between what is required overall to survive economically, to grow and prosper, and what the individuals in it need if they are to survive, grow and prosper.

Quality Circles form one aspect of the approach, which aims to serve everyone by developing that good fit. By participating in decisions about their work and by acquiring the knowledge that enables them successfully to do so, people derive more interest and satisfaction from their work, and the company benefits from their knowledge and experience.

Overview

May and Baker was quick to recognise the potential benefits of the Quality Circle approach, and was one of the first companies in Britain to introduce the concept. It chose to use a firm of consultants to assist it with their introduction and so it was in January 1980 that the company took the first steps with its Quality Circles programme. After a series of meetings designed to introduce the concept to everybody down to and including first-line supervision and also the trade union representatives, volunteers were sought for the first Quality Circle leaders' course. This was held successfully and as a result of this course five Quality Circles were set up on the Dagenham site. Over the ensuing two years this number rose to twenty-seven, of which the great majority were successful in achieving benefits ranging from improved communication and increased job satisfaction to considerable cost savings. It has not, of course, all been easy. The organisation has had much to learn about the concept and in many ways is still learning. Indeed, at the time of writing a major new initiative is being planned to expand the Quality Circle programme. This new initiative places Quality Circles firmly under the overall umbrella of the company's Quality of Working Life programme.

Looking back there is no doubt that the programme has been successful. Equally it could have been more so. As it is one of the longest-running Quality Circles programmes in the UK, it will be useful to explore the May and Baker experience, since this may be of benefit to organisations thinking of introducing the approach. Circles have been started up in many different locations and functions within the May and Baker organisation. Those which have been chosen to be included in the next section of this case history give an indication not only of the scope of the concept but also of some of the problems that they have faced and that other organisations are likely to face.

Examples of Quality Circles in action

The Pharmaceutical Bottle Inspection Quality Circle
This group was one of the original five Quality Circles set up in 1980. It is still in existence today and has gone through many different phases of development, from early enthusiasm, to confidence, to frustration and disruption due to organisational changes around it, and finally to maturity. The members of this Circle work in a formulation and packaging area of pharmaceutical production on the Dagenham site. The products they deal

with are used for injections and infusions and it is therefore essential that a very high standard of quality is maintained. Basically there are two sizes of bottle which they have to inspect, but a range of over twenty different products can be contained within the bottles. After being filled, the bottles are sterilised, allowed to cool and inspected. It is this highly-skilled process which is the specialisation of the members of the group. The area consists of ten female operators and one supervisor. The supervisor is responsible for the day-to-day routine and the overall organisation of work. After she had volunteered to attend the first Quality Circle leader course, the supervisor of the work area called a meeting in the section to launch the idea of forming a Quality Circle. All the operators were interested and they agreed to set up a Circle with seven members, leaving three to maintain workflow during meetings. It was immediately recognised that those not directly involved should always be kept informed of the Circle's activities. The Circle began its training and was able to identify eighty-eight problems in a twenty-minute brainstorming session held during one of its first meetings.

The first problem they chose to deal with was interesting for several reasons. Working as they did at a number of machines situated close together, the group had developed a high level of cohesiveness. When, as sometimes happened, one of the machines broke down, it was necessary to re-deploy members of the group. The normal way of doing this was to disperse the team over the rest of the factory to assist in whatever tasks needed doing in the other areas. This caused frustration amongst the Quality Circle team, since they felt that it adversely affected their team spirit. In the early days the Circle might have been tempted to go to management simply to ask if they could be left together as a team. Had they done so they would have taken with them only their opinions, their feelings, their reactions; and almost inevitably their request would have been rejected. From the managerial point of view it would not have been good practice to have people standing idle and possibly disrupting the rest of the work while a machine was being repaired. The fact that the group did not choose this route is a tribute not only to them but also to the training that Quality Circles gives it members. Because of the concentration on data-based problem-solving, the group was quick to see the weakness of its first reaction. The members did not, however, give up since they recognised that both time and production were lost when the machines broke down. Their objective therefore changed from being a social one of keeping the group together because it was not pleasant being apart, to a tangible and hard-nosed objective, that of saving time and production normally lost in the area due to machine breakdown.

The first stage of their investigation was to collect data about machine performance. The team worked on four machines and they collected data about the performance of each of these machines over a thirty-five-day period. They designed the checksheets themselves, and decided how the group was to collect the data. Since these products were much in demand, any downtime represented a loss not only of time but also of revenue to the company, and the group became very interested and concerned to find a solution to this problem. Further analysis of the data they had collected revealed that two machines, in fact the older two, were particularly vulnerable to breakdown. These two machines were also the slower ones, and the group began to investigate the possibility of inspecting the bottles by hand if the machines broke down. They ran some tests and, to their surprise, they found that they could inspect bottles by hand faster than the two older machines, especially over short periods of time. From this the solution seemed clear, that they should build an inspection booth in an unused part of the factory floor which would allow them to inspect manually.

The group became very excited at the prospect of having solved this problem, and some informal soundings were made amongst the managers. It quickly became clear from these that the solution was not possible, because of the constraints imposed by Good Manufacturing Practice, which is the code imposed on manufacturers of pharmaceutical products. A part of this code states that once a product has been positioned on the factory floor it must not be moved 'unconventionally', so as to avoid any danger of mixing up the products. The group's reaction to this setback was predictable; they were very disappointed and began to wonder whether their managers really were committed to the work of their group. They were not entirely discouraged, however, and they decided to use the technique of brainstorming in an attempt to resolve this latest difficulty. As a result of this brainstorming session the group produced a novel and creative solution. In effect, they said, if we cannot take the products to the hand-inspection booth, why not bring the hand-inspection booth to the products? Their solution to the problem was, therefore, to design and build a mobile hand-inspection booth which would be brought into their work area when any of their machines broke down and would be used by any of the team to maintain the flow of production while the machine was being mended.

This solution was enthusiastically greeted by management, who saw in it potential for reducing lost time and improving production levels as well as maintaining and improving the morale of the workgroup. The management presentation which was prepared by this Quality Circle detailed the cost of the mobile inspection booth as £300, and the benefit of increased production of much-needed products conservatively estimated at a quarter of a million pounds per annum. It is not only the scale of the benefits that makes this particular Quality Circle project interesting; it is the way they tackled the problem, specifically the difference between opinion-based argument on the one hand, which is the way that they were initially intending to present their views, and the data-based arguments on the other hand which fortunately they chose to use. It would have been very easy for management to have argued against the opinions of the group, especially those relating to their desire to stay together as a group, but it was difficult for them to refute the data-based case presented. Indeed, the managers concerned were delighted with the potential benefits which the group identified.

Having achieved this early success the Circle became very confident and were justifiably proud of their achievement. They went on to tackle a number of other problems, including a method of handling bottles on and off the inspection machines, the causes and effects of rejected work, and the requirement for effective operator training on the job. Looking back on those early days the supervisor also recalls that Circle members not only worked hard during the Circle meetings, but that their attitude to their routine work in the area changed; they became more positive and co-operative and generally the team took a greater interest.

After the Quality Circle programme had been in existence for one year a review was arranged, attended by the Managing Director and approximately 150 other managers. The review took the form of presentations from individual Quality Circles on their progress. The supervisor from the Bottle Inspection Area took the opportunity to relate her Circle's experiences. Part of her talk involved listing the top ten achievements of her group during the previous year. The list indicates the wide range of problems Quality Circles can and do solve, and it is as follows. It is not in any order of importance.

1   The mobile hand-inspection booth was created.
2   A music system was introduced into the area.
3   A full-time porter was employed in the area to assist with moving heavy trolleys.

4   Trolleys were fitted with new nylon wheels to make them easier to move.
5   A routine preventative maintenance scheme for the inspection machines was introduced.
6   Feedback and communication with local management were improved.
7   A new training programme for the development of job skills was introduced.
8   The change-over system between shifts was improved.
9   The rejected work is handled more effectively so that congestion is decreased.
10 The group was able to participate in discussions about the plans for moving into the new facility.

The whole review was videorecorded and her Circle saw the film. This was another large boost to the confidence of the group, and it would have been easy to have assumed that all would have been plain sailing from now on. This was not to be, however. During 1982, a number of significant problems arose in close conjunction with each other, which had a negative effect on the working of this group. For example, a number of key people involved in supporting the Circle either left the company or were transferred to other departments, all in the space of a few months. These were the second-line supervisor, the Department Head, the Quality Circle facilitator and the Quality Circle co-ordinator. Furthermore, there were delays in completing some of the alterations which the Circle had proposed, which led to frustration for the group. It was also at this time that the group became aware that a new style of facility was to be built by the company, which meant that the group would have to be relocated. As a result of these things the Circle members and their leader became very unsettled. Meetings were still held but they were not so effective. After a series of discussions between management and the Circle to try and restore confidence, the group decided to concentrate on problems involved in moving to the new building. In the interim, however, two members had left the Circle. This was disappointing, even though one was replaced by a new volunteer from the work area.

The decision to focus attention on the new work area and the injection of new blood into the group heralded a new period of positive action and results. Two and a half years later the Circle is still active, and furthermore it has developed in maturity to the extent that it can maintain its effectiveness without the rigid routine of meetings once every week. It has begun to take the step from Quality Circles being a one hour a week concept, to being something which is a normal part of 'the way we do things during our time at work'. This is in many ways the ultimate goal of any Quality Circle programme.

The Finance/Accountancy Quality Circle

Having dealt with a very successful group, it is perhaps only fair to balance it with one that failed. This Quality Circle was one of the later ones formed during 1981. The people concerned worked in two office areas and dealt with the preparation and checking of final accounts, including sales ledgers, cash management and supply ledgers. We were conscious from the start that the group came from more than one work area and that this might lead to a difficulty, but such was the level of interest and enthusiasm that it was decided to give them the opportunity. Seven people volunteered to start the group and during their brainstorming session they identified 25 problems, but they had difficulty identifying a work problem common to them all. Finally they decided to tackle 'time spent communicating with the Computer Department at the end of the month'. They approached this by analysing the work system, and they also assessed the viability of introducing a data link within the Department to avoid the necessity of having to walk to and from the computer building. The enthusiasm and commitment of the group were rapidly eroded, however, and after eight meetings the Circle folded without having given a management presentation.

Looking back on this experience it is possible to isolate a number of causes, some of which would have been difficult to avoid, but some which could have been handled more effectively. The first problem was that the group was started at the same time as an office reorganisation was taking place. Perhaps, with the benefit of hindsight, it would have been better to have delayed the start of the Circle until this reorganisation had been completed. Secondly, the members of the Quality Circle were actually representatives of two workgroups which were geographically remote. The lesson here is clear. The ground rules of Quality Circles state that the Circles consist of people working in the same area with the same supervisor. We had recognised this, but had wanted to give the staff in the two areas their opportunity. In effect, this group was more of a project team than a Quality Circle and this seems to have been the main reason for their not finding it easy to identify common areas of concern.

The third difficulty faced by this group was a change of staff at supervisory level during the first two months of the Quality Circle's life. When this happens, as it invariably will from time to time, it is essential that the group and the new supervisor confront the issue, recognise the voluntary nature of the approach and come to a mutually agreeable decision as to what should be done. This did not happen in this case.

Fourthly, the problem that the group decided to tackle was a rather diffuse and general one. This is always more likely to happen when a group is set up with members from more than one work area. In circumstances such as these the normal tendency of any group is to move towards more general themes and problems and to move away from tangible, specific day-to-day difficulties which they themselves can tackle. The danger here, of course, is that the more general and diffuse the problem the more difficult it is to tackle with any degree of tangible success. Communication problems are a good example of this phenomenon.

So this particular Quality Circle was not successful. It is important, however, to note that the lack of success of this group was in no way connected to the work area that they came from. The approach works just as well in office environments as it does in production line situations and indeed many others.

The third example of a Quality Circle comes from the Quality Control function and is a good demonstration of this point.

The Pharmaceutical Quality Control Quality Circle

This work area consists of a chemical laboratory linked to the pharmaceutical production area. The staff here are responsible for the quality control of all pharmaceutical products, including capsules, suppositories, tablets, creams, and elixirs. An interesting early feature of this group is that all sixteen members of staff in the section volunteered to join the Quality Circle. This number is outside the guidelines usually recommended for Quality Circle groups, which suggest a maximum membership of about ten. The whole section was involved in the decision about how to handle this difficulty, and they decided that they would rotate attendance at Circle meetings. This meant that work in the laboratory could continue during Circle meetings, but also that everyone who wanted to could remain involved.

During their initial brainstorming session they were able to identify 66 problems which they divided into five main themes. The first problem they decided to tackle was 'the wastage of samples'. A large element of their work was to receive samples from Production, to test them, and thereby be able to recommend acceptance or rejection of the whole batch from which the samples were derived. Any unused samples are destroyed. The Circle began with the belief that the size of samples brought in from Production was too large and could be reduced but still be representative of the whole batch. After a period of data collection the group was ready to give a presentation to management which was both detailed and highly analytical, as would be expected from staff in this work area. The basis of their recommendation was that sample sizes could be reduced and that this would lead to a reduction in wastage and therefore a financial saving. They calculated that it was possible to save between four and five thousand pounds per annum by solving this problem. Their suggestions were accepted and implemented by management.

Problems

It would be unrealistic to think that a concept which encourages staff and managers to change their work habits significantly either by joining a Quality Circle or by modifying their managerial style to encourage such groups to start up would be introduced and maintained without some difficulties. This has been the case in May and Baker and it may be useful to other organisations contemplating a programme for us to explore the main problems which arose. The first concerns the resourcing of the programme, a subject which is of crucial importance.

There is no doubt that our failure to maintain an adequate level of facilitator back-up had a detrimental effect on the programme for a while. Looking back it is easy to see that there was no natural focus for Circle leaders and members to turn to, no one to help the training and development process which is essential, especially to 'young' groups. There is a serious requirement for one or more people to commit themselves to helping the groups, 'oiling wheels' where necessary and planning the future development of Quality Circles. It should not be forgotten that the introduction of this concept represents a serious change in the working life of those who take part, and it is unrealistic to expect that it will be accomplished without support and guidance. This situation has now been remedied by the appointment of a full-time co-ordinator, although there was a gap of several months before this occurred.

The second difficulty faced related to the fact that the aforementioned reorganisation was preceded by a voluntary early retirement scheme which affected the Quality Circle membership, particularly at the supervisory level. Any change in membership can be unsettling but a change in leadership particularly so. Of course it is difficult to predict the future, but we now believe that situations such as this should be countered by ensuring an increase in the support and encouragement given to the groups. A basic tenet of the Quality Circles approach is that they must live in the real world. There are no magic wands either to solve the problems or to guard against outside circumstances, and a task of the facilitator is to help groups and individuals understand this.

As has been said before, the interest in Quality Circles is encouragingly high throughout the company. As might be expected with a voluntary approach, however, the interest and commitment is not universal. Indeed, attitudes towards the concept vary from the very negative to the totally positive. This is reflected at most levels in the organisations, but is highlighted amongst middle management. This is very important since the attitude of the middle manager has an immediate and lasting effect on the Quality Circle. At the outset the groups themselves very often point to this, and express their hope that their manager will support their efforts. The two main areas of concern amongst some middle managers which sometimes lead to sceptical and negative attitudes are, firstly, that many of them have seen various 'new' management techniques introduced, only apparently to be replaced within a year or so by the next fashion. It is not entirely surprising, therefore, that some managers will initially view Quality Circles in the same light. At May and Baker we are doing everything we can in an attempt to demonstrate that Quality Circles, and the whole of our Quality of Working Life programme, are here to stay. It takes time and there is a continuing need to stress the lasting commitment of the company. We are confident that we will succeed.

The second reason we have found that sometimes causes anxiety and negativity amongst middle managers is fear that the approach will threaten their managerial status. Again it is important to remind ourselves of the scale of the change. It is natural that some will feel anxious and will therefore be unwilling to allow groups to start up in their department. Their wishes must always be respected and efforts made to demonstrate in a practical way, in areas where Quality Circles are formed, that they do not threaten management status, indeed that they very positively add to it through the improved morale, better teamwork, commitment and problem solving at staff level. Experience shows that Quality Circles put forward practical, fact-based solutions which are welcomed by local management, who are then happy to give authorisation to implement. On the occasions when a proposal is not acceptable the manager, who always receives the minutes of Quality Circle meetings, is able to talk to the group informally and demonstrate the difficulty. On the odd occasion when he does not intercept the proposal, the groups are almost always willing to accept counter arguments to their own, given that they are data-based and present a better case.

On the whole, at May and Baker we believe that the problem of scepticism is best tackled by constant encouragement to 'give it a go' and by demonstrating through existing groups that the concept does not threaten or demean managers, indeed quite the opposite. We know now, however, that this whole issue is something which requires a lot of time and effort in a company of our size. We believe that the effort is well worthwhile, and our Quality Circles programme, which is over three years old at the time of writing, testifies to this.

Evaluation

At May and Baker we have been concerned to evaluate our Quality Circle programme, not in the sense of checking up on the financial return, but more in terms of how different levels of staff view the programme. This gives us data which help to maintain and improve the effectiveness of the initiative. To this end we have undertaken two major surveys to test opinions. One was conducted during the first half of 1981 and the other in late 1982.

The first survey showed that the general evaluation of the programme was favourable. Circle members were quite strongly positive, as one might expect, with qualified support on occasions. Non-members had a favourable though lukewarm response mixed with a fair degree of scepticism about the programme. They did not oppose Circles, however.

It may be useful to show some of the relevant figures which the survey produced and these are produced below.

1 Overall

As overall indicators of people's attitudes we asked everyone (i) whether they saw Quality Circles are being in the best interests of all employees, (ii) whether they felt Circles had come up with really useful ideas for improving the way work is done.

(i) *Question* Do you feel that Quality Circles serve the best interest of the employees?

	Members	Non-members
Definitely	37%	10%
Sometimes	60%	86%
Total	97%	96%

(Remainder say Quality Circles do not serve employees' interests or do not know)

(ii) *Question* In your opinion have Quality Circles come up with any really useful ideas to improve the way work is done?

	Members	Non-members
Many	52%	10%
Some	39%	48%
Total	91%	58%

(Remainder say no useful ideas or do not know)

These results show that most non-members choose the positive alternatives from the range of possible answers to both questions, but opt for those which give lukewarm approval ('sometimes', 'some'). Over half believe Circles produce some useful ideas, though 58 per cent in total is not especially high. Circle members are far more positive in their appraisal on both issues.

2 Human relations
One of our interests was to see how far Circles have improved the climate of human relations in the firm. We believe they have had some success. More than half the people (61 per cent of members; 52 per cent of non-members) believe that Circles have improved relations between management and employees. We asked Circle members several further questions, the replies to which show how Circles have improved communication in the company.

64% report that they know more of what goes on in the firm.
74% report more understanding of the foremen's problems.
67% report more understanding of managers' problems.

52% feel the company is a better employer now that it consults about working methods.

Our own impression is that improvements in human relations result from three things.

(i)   Circles are seen as genuine attempts by management to draw on the experience which all employees feel they have.

(ii) Management is seen to be committed to Circles and does not regard them as a gimmick or a passing fashion. In this context it should be noted that about 70 per cent of both groups say that departmental and top management are really interested in taking up suggestions from the Circles.

(iii) Circles provide employees with more information than they would otherwise receive, although this is still not seen as sufficient, as was indicated in the replies to the general questions.

3   Frustrated expectations

One potential drawback of Circles is that they raise people's expectations, which may then be dashed by a negative response from management. We have just noted that managerial support was seen to be strong. We asked Circle members if they were satisfied with the reception their suggestions received, in particular whether they got satisfactory reasons if a proposal was turned down. Thirty-one per cent said no proposal had been turned down or they had not yet made any proposals; 42 per cent said they were satisfied with the reasons; 24 per cent said they were not satisfied. There was no widespread dissatisfaction, although the last figure is quite a significant minority.

4   Advantages for employees

When Circles improve efficiency by reducing costs or improving quality the company obviously benefits. In the long run employees may share these benefits to the extent that the company is more prosperous and can provide greater job security and afford higher wages. But Quality Circles may perhaps benefit members and other employees in another way, because they have the potential to improve jobs and working conditions and they are a means by which people may gain more influence over their working environment. Some people told us early on that May and Baker was interested only in improvements which cut costs and would ignore suggestions that might make employees' jobs easier. We checked this in the questionnaire. People see as May and Baker's main reason for introducing Quality Circles the desire to cut costs and find more efficient methods. Nevertheless, most (67 per cent) believe the company would be as receptive to ideas which improve jobs and conditions as to ideas which save costs or improve quality. We then asked if Circles had provided people with more say in how work is done in their section. Seventy-five per cent of members think they can have more say whereas only 35 per cent of non-members believe the Circle members do indeed have more say. So far as making jobs easier, about half (47 per cent) of the members and a fifth (18 per cent) of non-members think that this is so. Forty-six per cent of members say that they find working for the company more interesting and enjoyable since they have become Circle members.

These results indicate that members feel they have gained some worthwhile benefit in addition to any increased efficiency for the company. The general tone of remarks made in various informal discussions was that Circles give people a greater involvement in their work and provide them with an opportunity to improve their working conditions, but within fairly restricted limits. Non-members are very sceptical about such issues.

5 A 'high trust' strategy

To obtain one hundred per cent of the benefits possible

133

from a Quality Circles programme, people have to trust the company absolutely, believe that management and other employees share the same objectives, and feel that management will protect the interests of everyone in the firm. The general replies mentioned earlier show that May and Baker is seen as a good firm to work for, but that people do not feel that there is a complete unity of interest. In our view this attitude spills over into the assessment of Quality Circles, for example 81 per cent of Circle members are doubtful that they would pass on to management information about improvements which would reduce manning levels.

6 Insiders and outsiders

The questionnaire shows that this may be a problem, since 80 per cent of Circle members report that there may be some difficulty in persuading their colleagues not in the Circle to support changes suggested by the Circle.

7 Setting-up the programme

Members are satisfied with the way the programme has been organised and 85 per cent say that the training was good.

In the more recent survey amongst employees at all levels, almost two-thirds felt that the programme was designed to enhance their achievement and job satisfaction, and 28 per cent felt that the aim was to develop their potential and enhance productivity. Seventy-three per cent of team members said that Quality Circles had already produced benefits and the same proportion said that they would produce more in the future.

The great majority of members also believe that Quality Circles can help to improve communication between themselves and their managers and supervisors.

Eighty-five per cent of people said that Quality Circles were either useful or necessary for improving the quality of working life, and 83 per cent said they were useful or necessary in maintaining a Quality of Working Life programme. May and Baker is encouraged by these results, which indicate clearly that good progress has been made.

Summary
During the three years of the Quality Circle programme there have been setbacks. Due to company reorganisation and loss of key personnel the programme suffered badly at one stage. The lesson to be learnt from this is that any Quality Circles programme needs constant support throughout all levels of the organisation.

There are still areas of the company in which Quality Circles are not active. In these areas, though there are varying degrees of scepticism, all the evidence points to direct involvement being the best way of eliminating this, and progress is being made, even if only slowly, to maintain and expand commitment.

A significant new effort is now being made to expand our progress into new areas. This will involve a further concentrated training programme, to help with which the company is fortunate to have a team of highly committed facilitators spread over all the major sites.

May and Baker is convinced of the many advantages of its Quality Circle programme and feels that with the continued support of their employees at all levels and the active help of the trade unions, which they have been fortunate to have from the beginning, there is every reason to be confident of this programme's going from strength to strength in the future.

Suspending Quality Circles: Alcan Plate

John Bank

Quality Circles at Alcan are suspended at the time of writing. Management at the plant speaks of the programme as having been a 'qualified success', and members of the suspended QCs are keen to restart them. There is considerable positive feeling about the experience. The company has enjoyed both tangible benefits from Circles and a boost in morale during difficult times. Circle members have had the satisfaction of sorting out some of their problems and have tasted a few remarkable successes. There is energy to get Quality Circles going again.

Even in other companies where Quality Circle programmes seem to be outright failures, evidence shows that the majority of the people involved are willing to try again. In a study by B. Dale and S. Hayward, 76 per cent of the companies proposed to revive failed Circles. The main causes of failure revealed in the study were:

> rejection of the concept by top management and trade unions;
> the disruption caused by redundancies and company restructuring, labour turnover, lack of co-operation from middle and firstline managers and failure by Circle leaders to find enough time to organise meetings.

Companies that restart suspended Quality Circles often must get back to basics. Quality Circles are in fact quite simple, but there are key principles that are neglected at one's peril. These principles include the use of frontline supervisors as leaders, training of facilitators, Circle leaders and members, self-sufficiency of Circles, ownership of their problems, and regular, fixed meeting times.

Since the Circles are based on the natural workgroup, it is quite understandable that normally frontline supervisors are the Circle leaders. These Circle leaders, the members, and the facilitators all need special training in problem solving techniques and working together in groups. Training should be a permanent feature, with additional inputs being provided progressively as the groups develop their skills in diagnosis and analysis.

The training that the facilitators receive should include some advice on 'letting go' of the Circle. Their goal is to get the Circles to a stage|of self-sufficiency. They must be willing to step back and let the group go on its own way using the training it has been given.

This is often more difficult to do than it appears, but it is vital for the success of the group itself and the programme overall. If it does not happen there is a danger that the ownership of the group transfers from the members to the facilitator, or – a more serious one – that the facilitator becomes a surrogate line manager. As a rule of thumb, the facilitator should be able to start withdrawing from the average group after three to six months, and should more or less be clear of the group after six to nine months. If it takes longer than this, it does not necessarily mean that too much dependency is being built in, but it will certainly be worth asking the question.

Preparing for an £11.5 million expansion, while many other manufacturing firms in the Midlands were contracting, put Alcan Metal in an enviable position in the spring of 1981. It seemed a very good time to launch Quality Circles.

Background

ALCAN is the short name for Alcan Aluminium Limited of Canada, a multinational based in Montreal, whose main business is aluminium, from the mining of ore to the production and sale of numerous finished products. It has gross assets of over US$6.4 billion. Alcan Aluminium (UK) employs about 7,000 people in Britain and operates one of the only two major aluminium smelters left in the United Kingdom.

Alcan Plate Limited's works and offices are in Kitts Green (Birmingham). It now employs about 700 people, who are engaged in the manufacture and sales of plate products and the rolling of special sheet products. At the time of the Quality Circle launch the workforce numbered 1,000.

Production of aluminium has continued at Alcan Plate since 1938, when the company operated the plant to meet the needs of aircraft production during World War II. Throughout the years, the works has been continually modernised and the company has invested many millions of pounds in major plant and equipment since the late 1950s and early 1960s. Alcan Plate is the only source of aluminium plate in Britain and one of three large plants in Europe.

The works receives aluminium ingot and coil from other companies and converts this into a variety of semi-finished products by rolling and other methods. In recent years the company has been associated with, and supplied the metal for, a number of prestige products.

Almost all the major British aircraft – including the Anglo-French Concorde – have incorporated Alcan metal in their structure. The company currently provides material for the Trident, European Airbus, RAF Nimrod, the multi-role combat aircraft Tornado, the Jaguar and the Harrier, as well as many others. The Scorpion aluminium tank uses plate from Alcan. The European spacelab also required Alcan's aluminium plate.

A wide variety of high-technology plate produced by Alcan is also utilised in the shipbuilding industries. Ironically, Alcan aluminium plate was used both in HMS *Coventry* and HMS *Sheffield* and in the Exocet missiles that sank both ships during the Falklands war. Alcan produces coated strip aluminium for engineering markets and for cladding mobile homes and for use as architectural building sheets. For the domestic market,

Alcan supplies circles from which saucepans and kettles can be pressed and spun. This domestic side of the business and the market for coated strip aluminium was very depressed in the spring of 1981. The backbone of Alcan Plate – the military and aircraft market – was buoyant but becoming more fiercely competitive.

Convergences

The thrust to set up Quality Circles came from two separate sources. On the technical side, both Graham Johnson, Quality Supervisor, and his immediate superior, Brian Simons, Quality Manager, had read about Quality Circles and Johnson attended a half-day conference about them. They were keen to start pilot Circles.

Quite independently, Colin Siddle, Training Manager, and David Gregson, Personnel Manager, had initiated a training intervention for middle managers which dealt primarily with superintendents. The management development programme was undertaken in parallel with the extensive investment programme coming on stream. One of the concerns of senior management on site was to ensure that managers at all levels operated fully and consistently with their positions. It was observed that managers tended to drift to tasks and roles below their levels. A modular course was designed at the Cranfield School of Management to re-focus the superintendents and to counter the downward drift of managerial activity. Projects undertaken at the plant were linked to the learning modules at the business school. One of these projects was for the superintendents to help Graham Johnson launch a pilot programme of Quality Circles.

The decision to launch the Quality Circles was taken at Board level just before Easter in 1981. Early in April, the superintendents attended a five-day management development module at Cranfield. Quality Circles was one of the topics discussed. At the end of the module the men selected the introduction of Quality Circles at Alcan

Plate as their project to be effected between 9 April and their next module at Cranfield on 20 September. My role was to design the academic inputs at Cranfield and to supervise the on-site project work which was intended to give practical expression to the formal learning. The Quality Circles project seemed a perfect choice, as it encompassed many ideas of effective employee participation and good industrial relations.

By late June the preparation for the launch of Quality Circles was well under way. The superintendents working with Graham Johnson had selected a strategy for introducing the concept of Quality Circles. They used the 'portakabin' communication centre, affectionately called 'the Wendy House', to reach the workforce in small groups with a showing of a film on Quality Circles from British Leyland. No outside Quality Circle consultancies were employed. No formal training in Quality Circles was given to either foreman or Circle members. The company was intent on growing its own Circles using only its own resources, and this later proved to be a weakness in the programme.

Avoiding a crisis

Although it is desirable to 'grow your own' Quality Circles, there are certain core principles that emerge from the data on successful Circles programmes, for example, voluntariness and the *training* of Circle members, which are ignored at a company's peril. Alcan kept the programme voluntary, but the superintendents were on the verge of violating several other key principles.

Towards the end of June, on a visit to the works, I saw the superintendents' action plan for implementing the first two pilot Quality Circles. It contained errors about which I had to confront the men.

In retrospect, it had been quite naïve of me to expect that they would absorb the various readings and lectures I had given them on Quality Circles and extracted for themselves the principles needed for an effective launch. They had no expert input, nor had they been to visit Quality Circles in other companies. Not surprisingly, the plan the superintendents showed me contained three fundamental errors.

1   They wanted to hand down the initial problems for the Circles to solve, rather than let the Circles select the problems themselves. This would affect the 'ownership' of the problems. It also affected the level of trust in the Circle members, particularly when linked with the desire of superintendents to attend Circle meetings happening on their 'patch'.
2   They had decided to give some 'chairmanship' training to the foreman, and *no* Quality Circles training to the foreman or to Circle members.
3   They were over-reacting to an initial rebuff from the craft trade unions.

The trade union issue was by far the most immediate. At short notice, the superintendents had invited six representatives from the craft trade unions to an introductory session on Quality Circles at the plant communications centre. The short session was to consist of the showing of a film on Quality Circle introduction at British Leyland.

The initial response of the trade unionists to the face-to-face invitations was positive. They all said they would be there. But at the appointed time, not one trade union leader came. At first the superintendents' response was emotional. 'Well, they've had their bite of the cherry', one of them said, 'they'll not get another. We'll do it without them.' Fortunately, cooler heads prevailed and the trade union representatives were approached again.

It should not be surprising that trade unions are guarded and suspicious about Quality Circles. In 1981, few unions had policy statements about Quality Circles. The only document from the TUC appeared on 29 April

1981. That three-page document simply summarises the development of Quality Circles and their main features as a management technique. It offers some reasons for management interest in the technique and then gives a trade union response.

Searching for the motivation of companies in installing Quality Circles, the TUC paper says:

> Two factors are of prime importance in explaining why so many UK employers are experimenting with QCs. In the context of a general loss of competitiveness of their products, many UK employers have identified quality as a major problem, especially where an increasing market share is being taken by Japanese competitors. Attention has not surprisingly turned to Japanese quality control methods, and hence to QCs. The presence of automative and electronic components manufacturers among leading UK pioneers of QCs reflects this. Secondly, facing declining profitability and a need to cut costs, some employers have seen QCs as an area where significant savings can be made.
>
> QCs have the additional attraction that they involve the workforce in remedying these problems. They can thus be presented as a form of 'participation' – in answer to critics of British employers' autocratic style of management – while leaving managerial authority intact. For example, QCs' tight focus on quality problems alone makes them significantly less of a threat to 'management's right to manage' than established joint consultation systems on trade union machinery.

The TUC goes on to make a rather insightful comment.

> Trade unions have been urging employers for decades to give workers more control over the jobs they do. QCs are a belated recognition of

employees' expertise and knowledge and the need to put them to use. At the same time, trade unionists may be understandably sceptical about the merits of the latest in a succession of 'vogue' management techniques.

The document concludes with the caveats that QCs should not undermine existing trade union procedures or working methods, or be used to bypass existing trade union machinery, but that management should not keep all the benefits of QCs to itself either.

Industrial relations at Alcan Plate were running smoothly in 1981. The main unions on site were the Transport and General Workers Union (T & GWU) with two-fifths of the blue-collar workforce, and the balance divided among the Amalgamated Union of Engineering Workers (AUEW), the Electrical, Electronic, Telecommunications and Plumbing Union (EETPU) and the National Union of Sheet Metal Workers, Coppersmiths, Heating and Domestic Engineers (NUSMWCH & DE). Staff belonged to the Association of Scientific, Technical, Managerial and Supervisory Staffs (ASTMS) or the Association of Clerical, Technical and Supervisory Staffs (ACTSS).

The introduction of continuous shiftworking (the continental shift) had earlier met trade union opposition, but management had prevailed without building up a legacy of hostility. A renegotiation of the bonus system in the winter of 1981 to bring it into line with the company's profits rather than tonnage of production went surprisingly well. The main union involved in the Quality Circle installation was the T & GWU.

Start-up

The two pilot Quality Circles were begun in the plate finishing department and in the paint line section in late August. Because Alcan Plate works a continuous shift system, the meetings were held every twelve days at the start of the day shift for the Circle members.

Ken Smith, general foreman in the plate finishing department, became the first QC leader. He summed up the launch. 'Initial reactions were the same as in the past: "Well, it's another meeting and it will die a death." We got volunteers which included the shop steward who came to only one meeting but continued to give his support.' The QC in the Plate Finishing Department decided, as its first problem, to improve the surface quality of magnesium (non-heat-treatable) plate. Alcan had a bad reputation for surface quality in the market-place for customers looking for scratch-free, decorative finish on magnesium plate. The company's plate tended to be pitted and scratched, which was alright for machining or forming, but unsatisfactory if the customer planned to leave it as it came from the factory.

The QC produced a dozen solutions to the problem of surface scratches. These included using vacuum beans to handle the large wide plates, the use of foil to protect overlaps at annealing, and the use of card as protection when getting shoes across plate. The QC instigated the use of 2' × 2' wooden spacers (offcuts from cases that are used in another department) between the large sheets of metal at the stacking on the stretcher and did other practical things such as putting felt on rest plates and fitting more air wipes to blow swarf more successfully off the plate – all in an attempt to eliminate or reduce surface scratches. The basketful of ideas produced a 25 per cent lower rejection rate for surface defects as compared to the preceding six months, saving 3.36 tonnes of plate. In a period when customers were driving up inspection standards, this produced a direct saving (in 6 months) of £1,200 and an unquantifiable advantage in the market as the quality of Alcan magnesium plate began to rival that of its competitors.

Graham Johnson credits the QC with a 'dramatic improvement' in the surface quality of the magnesium plate. 'We went from horrible surfaces for non-heat-treatable magnesium to quite presentable surfaces as good as any in Europe and our salesmen felt the improvement immediately. This was directly attributable to the Quality Circle.' He explained, 'The Circles enabled us to get closer to the guys, to feed them information about the problems and the implication. They came up with ideas and ways of solving the problems. They asked for more information and this increased their overall interest in the job.'

The second pilot Quality Circle was started in the paint line with K. Rider as leader. Its first project was to improve the Tannoy system to effect speedier line communications. This proved to be an important project because a five-minute delay can cost up to 400 kg of scrap. During its first meeting the Circle also decided to improve on line viewing facilities which helped to spot paint defects.

Two further Circles were started – another in Plate Finishing and one in the Foundry. The Foundry Circle had the most dramatic first project, which registered savings of £15,000 per year.

The project was aimed at reducing melt loss. In the foundry casting furnaces, process scrap, raw ingots of aluminium and the necessary alloying elements are combined together and melted in one of three large casting furnaces. After the molten metal has been fluxed and cleansed it is cast into slabs or ingots by the semi-continuous Direct Chill method. At all stages in the process samples are taken for quality control purposes to ensure that the metal is of the correct alloy composition and of the highest quality.

During the melting process the dross rises to the top and is dragged off with rakes. Alcan Plate used to pay an outside firm to take away the dross, reclaim good aluminium metal and then sell the metal back to Alcan. The Quality Circle in the Foundry took on this problem of melt loss, solved it, and was able to dispense with the services of the outside firm. The Circle then began to look at ways of improving draining and preserving spillage scrap as a usable commodity. The suggestions they came up with and implemented included:

1 Designing small dross pans with holes to drain holder dross after fixing it with a flux. (The flux makes the dross cling to it, and when the flux is raked into an atmosphere with more oxygen it flares up again, releasing the aluminium.)
2 Developing spillage pans for scrap.
3 Using serrated rakes (instead of straight-edge ones) to reduce the amount of metal being skimmed off along with the dross.
4 New procedures for charging pellets.

The use of the small dross pans alone is saving about 28 kg of metal every time a furnace is charged. This is worth over £15,000 per annum.

Fighting for survival
Despite the initial success, circumstances at Alcan Plate conspired against QCs. There were the problems of installing the new furnace and computer systems. Furthermore, a sharp downturn in the market forced about 300 redundancies on the already small workforce. ('The way the market has gone, the metal you can sell is the hardest to produce and has the lowest revenue return', Graham Johnson said.) The redundancies took away the attention of management which was necessary for Quality Circles to thrive. As Graham Johnson explained in the autumn of 1983, 'When you go through a large redundancy programme you tend not to adjust immediately. You don't gear down straight away, you try to carry on providing the information and services you did before. We now must learn to adjust. During the last nine months we've not had time for Circles so they've been suspended. But we are now planning a relaunch. We want one in each department on each shift.' The

excessive dependency of the Circle on the two managers, Graham Johnson and Ken Smith, meant they could not operate without the men in attendance.

Circle members at Alcan were keen to get under way again after the nine-month suspension. They kept coming to Graham Johnson and Ken Smith to ask when the next meeting would be. They also kept approaching management with their ideas.

The relaunch of Quality Circles at Alcan Plate will benefit from hindsight. Circle leaders and members will have basic training in problem solving. The Circle leaders will be, not the general foremen, but the front-line foremen. They will also be developed with less dependency on higher management being involved in the running of the meetings. The aim will be for greater Quality Circle competence through training and more operational autonomy.

Success critique

Graham Johnson, Ken Smith and the superintendents do not consider the Quality Circle programme at Alcan Plate a failure. It is rather a 'qualified success'. They hope to adjust their ideas on Quality Circles a little, drawing on their two years' experience with them.

Studies of QC programmes in the USA and Canada suggest that there are five common reasons for failure.

1 Not preparing the organisation for change
The transition from an autocratic management style to a participative one is far-ranging. It requires changes in attitude and behaviour from the top to the bottom of the organisation. Unless a company is willing to fit Quality Circles into a framework of genuine employee participation and involvement, chances of success are slim.

Particular attention must be paid to supervisors and middle managers, who may see the introduction of Quality Circles as a threat to their power and authority. Actually in genuine participation programmes no one loses power. There is a power-rise for everyone in the system as communications improve up and down the organisation, problems are solved at appropriate levels and shared decision-making becomes the normal way of doing things. Quality Circles then become a vital part of the new form of employee involvement.

2 Isolated problem solving
Circles can fail if their problem-solving focus fails to take account of knock-on effects and interface problems. Unless a QC holds fast to the principles of 'putting our own house in order' and 'no finger pointing', it may tackle a problem that is not particular to its area and therefore not solvable by its members.

Sometimes a solution decided on by one QC could have an adverse effect on another department, a knock-on effect – that is negative for the company. It would be especially abrasive if one workgroup were to be applauded for a QC success which adversely affected another group. Hence the crucial role of the QC facilitator in anticipating interface problems.

3 Poor diagnosis
Superficial work by Quality Circles could focus on symptoms rather than root causes of problems. What may appear to be a communications problem in an office environment may actually be a role clarification problem. Were a QC to recommend communications training to deal with the problem instead of a clarification of roles and job standards, it would be wide of the mark. Many organisational problems must be examined from a systems or structural point of view rather than at workgroup level.

4 Undisciplined priority selection
QC groups often fall into the 'squeaky wheel trap' and deal first with problems raised by the most vocal employees or managers. Quieter problems affecting the

silent majority may be neglected as a Circle goes for a quick success. Good Circle leaders and facilitators should help Circles select problems according to definite criteria. For example, a six-question checklist might be used.

(i)   Is it a problem *we* can solve?
(ii) Can we solve it in a reasonable time (2–3 months)?
(iii) Will it help our QC training?
(iv) Can we collect data about the problem?
(v)   Is the solution cost-effective?
(vi) Do we really *want* to do it?

5 Not integrating all communication levels
Four interconnected levels of communication exist in organisations.

(i)   Organisation to outside environment.
(ii) Group to group.
(iii) Individual to group.
(iv) Individual to individual.

QC programmes often focus on the individual-to-group relationship and, if not careful, can become a closed club. Efforts must be made to keep all lines of communication open. Simple gestures like the posting of minutes and the sending of minutes to other managers and to trade union representatives are important. The organisation should be viewed as an interconnected system, with Quality Circles fully integrated into the system, for the Circles to be most effective.

Ed Kowaleski of the Ford Motor Company (USA) summed up the 4½-year experience of Quality Circles at Ford's in San Francisco, saying it took eighteen months to get results. The pay-off of the programme came in attitude change away from 'them and us' to more positive co-operation and participation. A similar attitudinal change brought on by Quality Circles came from the Alcan experience. In fact, Graham Johnson sees this as the primary achievement – to date – of Alcan Plate's QC programme. 'A Quality Circle', he said, 'is a tool with which I can get some help in changing people's attitudes. Even though we've stopped having meetings we've had employees saying "When's the next Circle meeting because I've got this idea?" . . . We've not had a meeting in over six months and they still flag problems and want to get going again. It's been almost a revolution and it had to happen or otherwise we'd have gone under. Now their attitude is amazingly positive and we cannot let Quality Circles drop.'

Part II
DEALING WITH PROBLEMS

Sustaining Quality Circles

Organisations often ask how Quality Circles are maintained, either after the first flush of enthusiasm has died away, when there are newer and more immediate pressures on people's time, or when the problems have all been solved. It is an important question and one which the concept must answer if it is to live up to its claim of being a lasting approach.

Perhaps the most important point to stress about this question is that Quality Circles represents a part of a managerial philosophy. This means that it is part of the basic system of beliefs and assumptions held by the organisation and therefore commitment to it should not falter after a month, a year or a decade. Many companies, however, become worried after a short time when the initial gloss has worn off, even though in fact this stage represents the end of the beginning rather than the beginning of the end. If people see the approach in the same light as a gimmick or fashion it is easy to understand their concern, since it is not possible to keep things entirely new for ever. Quality Circles is substantial enough, however, if managed well, and with appropriate underlying commitment and belief, to continue to grow and to prosper given almost any difficulty.

Rescuing a faltering QC programme

Before exploring some of the ways in which it is possible to manage the problem, we should establish when it is likely to occur. In practice there is more than one danger period, but the first is usually the most difficult to cope with, and this usually comes some time between one and two years after the launch. One of the difficulties of planning a Quality Circles programme lies in the opposite pulls of not rushing too much, rather building up the number of Circles gradually and carefully, and wishing to enable a 'critical mass' of people to join in as soon as possible, since this will help the overall programme to withstand the inevitable problems that will afflict one or two of the groups. Two important points about starting new Circles are that the rules of the approach must be observed at all costs, and that there must be adequate resourcing available, in the shape of a facilitator, to help the new groups to get off the ground.

Even after a year or so, in many organisations the approach will still be conducted on a relatively small scale, with maybe ten to fifteen groups operating, and if a 'recession' hits the programme at this time it can cause a lot of anxiety. It is necessary in circumstances such as these to recognise that in any programme there will be some groups that decide at some stage, and for one reason or another, to call it a day, maybe because they could not think of a compelling subject to work on, maybe out of some kind of frustration or even that they were not able to sustain their adherence to the rules of Quality Circles, and had relapsed into unproductive and frustrating finger pointing and opinion-based argument. Of course in all these cases the resident facilitator will have spent time and effort trying to help the group confront the problem. All the difficulties mentioned are soluble, but it must be recognised that occasionally Quality Circles find themselves unwilling or unable to confront the issues involved. In circumstances such as this, the guidelines to be adhered to are that the group should be allowed to discontinue, and that it should realise that it can begin again whenever the members and the leader want to; the door is always open. The key point here is that one or two groups folding up does not either mean or signal the end of the programme.

Any Quality Circles programme should have an active and carefully thought-through communication strategy, which should include 'advertising' both the concept itself and the successes of the groups. In the event of one or two groups falling by the wayside, it may be appropriate to use this medium to encourage more groups to form and thus to use all the available facilitator support.

Prevention better than cure
In the long run, Quality Circles depend on having a critical mass of people involved in them. This may be anything from 10 per cent to 50 per cent of the organisation, depending on the culture of the place, and it is important that the programme should develop to a stage where it can sustain itself without drama, even if one or two groups are having difficulties at any point in time. Rule One about sustaining a programme, then, is that the co-ordinator and facilitator should plan to be able to expand the programme, given sufficient volunteers, to achieve this within eighteen months or so.

Rule Two is to recognise that some groups will be successful enough ultimately for the remaining problems in their area to be so trivial that they are not very compelling to work on. It is important in situations such as this to remember that Quality Circles are not only there to deal with problems; they can look at any topic within their area that they believe they can influence positively. So it is as well, from the outset, to encourage groups to think about opportunities as well as problems. Once this happens, the lifespan of the group becomes virtually infinite, since there will always be possibilities of making things even better. A classic, and maybe apocryphal, example of this is that of the Japanese Quality Circle in the automobile industry who tried to knock a few minutes off the make-ready time for the machine they used. The internationally accepted standard for this activity was six hours and they happily worked to this norm and therefore did not have a problem. By working at it over a period of time they began to realise, however, that there was a big opportunity for them to improve and in the end they reduced the time to three minutes! No problem; but what an opportunity! It would not matter if the story were exaggerated, since it serves to demonstrate very lucidly the point at issue and facilitators should try from the outset to help Circles to consider the wide range of issues available to them to tackle, and not just the ones that are problems. This process should be built in from the beginning so that, once the main problems have been solved, the group can move more naturally into areas of opportunity.

Another guideline is that Quality Circles, with the help of their facilitator, will ultimately move to a situation wherein they are ready to tackle genuine interface problems with another group, and this obviously helps to broaden their scope. It is vital, however, that this move is not rushed, since if it is there will most likely be problems of finger-pointing rather than genuine problem solving between the groups concerned. The tendency towards finger-pointing is very strong in most organisations, and amongst many individuals, and it is essential therefore that individual Quality Circles work on putting their own house in order before any such move is made towards working on common problems with other groups. There is, of course, no absolute rule about how long it will take to encourage groups out of any bad habits; experience dictates, however, that it is unlikely to be less than a year and could be as long as two or three years. Rushing groups into the tackling of problems at the interface between departments is a serious mistake, however compelling it may seem at the time, and it will serve groups well to focus their attention on their training and their own problems at the start. Working group on group will evolve as a natural progression without being forced.

The final guideline for sustaining a programme is that effort should be made to integrate the Quality Circles process into 'the normal way we do things', for all the time at work. The initial requirement for meeting once a week and that meeting lasting for an hour helps people to get into the habit, and serves to provide a framework for training and for getting things done, but if the concept is working to its full potential people will be using the principles and practices of the approach during the whole of the working week. This is in contrast to the group in the shipbuilding industry which had been meeting for a couple of months. They were gathering together for their weekly meeting, which was held from 12.00 to 1.00 pm every Thursday, and one member in particular was lambasting the people in another section and calling them all the names under the sun. One of his colleagues in the Quality Circle interjected and said, 'Come on Harry, no finger-pointing!', at which point Harry looked at the clock on the wall and replied, 'No it's all right, I've got three minutes to go yet!' It is not easy to change the habits of a lifetime, but Quality Circles gives us the chance to become more positive, and this has to be worked on consistently and urgently. It is because of our frailty as human beings that groups should not hurry the move towards the more difficult and possibly emotive issues involved in group-on-group working, but nonetheless, at the appropriate time, this is an important development which sustains the freshness of the programme.

Finally, we must return to the central point, that Quality Circles forms part of an ongoing way of managing; it is not a 'throwaway' tool. Therefore these mechanisms for sustaining the programme will only work given the continuing commitment of the management structure to the concept.

How to fail with Quality Circles

It is notoriously difficult to get people and organisations to write about their failures. The case histories in this book have indicated areas of difficulty but it has to be accepted that most of the problems referred to were solved by the organisations in question and that the companies who have contributed their stories have had at least some success with the Quality Circles approach.

The right environment
It would be wrong, however, to conclude a book such as this without addressing some of the difficulties which arise, albeit outside the case history framework. Quality Circles is a more complex concept than it seems, and many organisations have failed to introduce and maintain it successfully. There are a variety of apparent reasons for this but by far the most common cause of failure is that the organisational culture did not really fit the approach. We have already stated that Quality Circles is a precise mechanism. It is not and does not intend to be a panacea. It can assist the process of organisational change towards a more open and participative style if the company concerned really is committed to achieving this change and is prepared to work at it over the long term. Equally Quality Circles can be one reflection of a company which already manages in this way. Quality Circles, however, cannot help an organisation to manage more autocratically; it cannot in the long term help to get

more for less out of an unwilling and ignorant workforce. It is unlikely that many organisations have introduced the concept with these two latter goals explicitly in mind, but many have verged on it and thereby caused the failure of their programme.

To understand this we need to go back to Douglas McGregor's Theory X and Theory Y. McGregor's study of the assumptions that people and organisations make about employees is one of the most talked-about topics in management training, and yet it is by far the least understood. Even more dangerous than this is the fact that many managers who do not properly understand and believe in the Theory Y approach still claim to do so. It is in this area that failures to sustain participative approaches such as Quality Circles occur.

McGregor talks about two conditions, which he labels Theory X and Theory Y. His book, *The Human Side of Enterprise*, was published in 1960. To understand organisations in the 1980s we need to add another category or, more accurately, to subdivide Theory X into two parts, which we can label 'Hard' and 'Soft'. When McGregor was researching his book in the 1950s there was significantly less social legislation than there is today. The constraints on hiring and firing were less complex and indeed less restrictive. Trade unions did not hold the powerful position and role that they currently enjoy. In investigating organisations McGregor discovered companies whose management style was 'exploitive authoritarian', to use Likert's phrase. Management that could and did say, 'Put up or shut up', and 'If you don't like it you know where the gate is!' Companies which behaved in this way led McGregor to describe a series of assumptions which he labelled Theory X: low expectations about people in general, and a belief that most people were lazy and uninterested and would therefore have to be bribed, threatened or coerced into any activity to achieve organisational objectives. Organisations like this 'knew' that people were not interested in responsibility, that they only wanted security.

The advent of the mass of legislation designed to protect the employee against exploitation, the rise in power of the trade unions and, it must be said, the awakening of a greater sense, amongst some people, of the value and dignity of the individual, have changed Theory X. Nowadays we rarely see the picture of the bowler-hatted foreman hiring and firing at will, and standing over his staff watching for the slightest sign of flagging. This does not, however, mean that Theory X has disappeared; not at all – it is alive and well, albeit changed to a different, more insidious form. In the past, at least there were no bones made about it; the assumptions being made were explicit and obvious. Workers worked for money and through fear of being summarily sacked. It was deemed to be as simple as that. Now, many organisations are on a constant search for ways to motivate their workforce.

Why? Because people are lazy and have to be coerced, bribed or threatened to put forth effort! Because you cannot expect anything else of people! Because they do not want responsibility! In other words, Theory X in a new 'soft' guise. Many such organisations regard themselves as genuinely participative and Theory Y, yet they are light years away from being so. Recently a senior executive of a progressive, multinational company in the food business which claims to be all that is progressive and enlightened in terms of management was asked about the applicability of Quality Circles within his division. He said, 'Oh no, not now. We are looking for the next flavour of the month, not the last one.'

A qualitative view of organisations indicates that considerably more Theory X than Theory Y is practised, although the number of organisations which manage in a genuinely open and participative way seems to be growing slowly. Autocratic management styles are in many ways the 'natural' way things have been done in the past, and as such are not easy to change. Indeed there may be situations where it is unwise to change them, certainly overnight. If people have been used to being treated autocratically it is dangerous to walk in one day and dramatically change the style. There is a need for caution and the gradual development of more open and participative approaches. We should remember that it is no easier to get out of the habit of being managed autocratically than it is to change the style itself, and it takes time, skill, care and commitment from everyone.

Many organisations have found it difficult to sustain their efforts to manage this kind of cultural change in their environments, and Quality Circles are as susceptible as any other approach in this situation. Because of this it will be useful and appropriate to establish some of the guidelines for those who wish to engage in this kind of activity. It is far better to delay starting, or not to start at all, than to begin with unrealistic expectations and not be able to match them.

Four helpful guidelines

Guideline One is that Quality Circles, and any other genuinely participative mechanism, involves a high level of trust in people within the organisation. The president of a major Japanese company said recently, 'Trust, train and inform your people and they will reward you many times.' Two points about this are essential. One is that trust is not a movable feast. It is no good saying that we trusted people yesterday but not today, or that we trust them with this information but not with that. Trust, like diamonds, has to be for ever. Equally, it is unrealistic to trust everyone with everything without precaution. We do not allow our eight-year-old sons to handle loaded firearms, or give our five-year-old daughters matches to play with. In these situations we develop our children to a state where trust is possible, through a process of training and informing. It is the same in organisations. Trust is only a realistic possibility given the training and information required to enable appropriate attitudes to be formed and high-quality decisions to be made.

Guideline Two, then, is that the process of training and informing is vital and that the requirement does not stop: it must become a central and permanent part of the organisation's culture. It is only through this that the necessary framework for trust can be built.

Guideline Three is that the whole process is a permanent one and that it is likely to be three to five years before an organisation reaches a point which could be called 'the end of the beginning', a point at which there is a basic and widespread belief in the commitment of the organisation to the principles and practice of open and participative management. From this point the discussion throughout all levels of the organisation moves away from 'do we trust them?' and 'will they really keep it up?', to an acceptance of the long-term commitment, and a constructive debate about the best mechanisms to employ. The problem here is that Western organisations tend to think in the short term. It is by no means as easy as it might appear to give the total commitment that is required to change the culture of a company and, more important, to maintain it. It is so easy for other issues and pressures to begin clouding the scene after six or more months, and for compromise rather than commitment to become the operative word.

Guideline Four is that change of the type being discussed affects the whole of the organisation. Quality Circles, for example, have as much to do with middle and senior management as they do with the supervisor and his staff. A mistake often made is to introduce changes into companies without recognising their full impact on the whole of the organisation. Quality Circles cannot operate successfully in the long term without the active commitment and support of the management structure above them, and many organisations would do well to devote time to the training and development of their managers before contemplating the introduction of

Quality Circles. By doing this a solid framework can be built within which managers recognise the potential of their staff and yet are not threatened by it because they begin to see their job involving the liberating and utilising of this resource.

This book is not intended as a comprehensive guide to the management of complex organisational changes as such and there are important aspects of this subject which we have not covered. The four guidelines do, however, point to some of the crucial issues and can aid understanding of failures to introduce and maintain Quality Circles successfully. They can also act as a caution to those about to decide whether or not to proceed.

Causes of failure

One of the chief causes of difficulty, then, with the Quality Circles approach was the failure of some companies to think fully through the meaning and implications of developing an open and participative style of management, of which Quality Circles is a part, and in not building commitment to it into the day-to-day behaviour of the organisation.

Another common cause of failure with the concept is the non-observance, either conscious or unwitting, of some organisations of the long-established 'rules' which underpin it. One leading manufacturer in the UK decided to introduce Quality Circles but to do it their own way. They broke the rule of voluntariness amongst their supervisors and decided to set up groups wholesale right from the beginning, and without any real consultation or agreement from their unions. The programme lasted only a few months. Over two years later the unions in question refuse even to talk about Quality Circles, which is sad since the organisation did not introduce Quality Circles, but pinned the label on a series of actions which were bound to fail. It is a classic case of not thinking through the implications of the concept and fitting it into

163

a coherent and explicit managerial philosophy.

The voluntary rule in Quality Circles is not there for fun or as a gimmick; it is an essential part of the approach. There are three reasons for this. Firstly, it is a demonstration of trust, that staff be given the choice of whether or not to join in. Secondly, it helps to place the ownership of the Circles where it should be, that is, with the groups themselves, and thirdly, it ensures a high level of commitment amongst those who do join in. No one can say that he is only doing it because he was told to.

The voluntary rule must apply, of course, at all levels of the organisation. It would be just as bad for a senior or middle manager to say that he only had Quality Circles in his area because he was forced to, as it would for a supervisor or a member of staff. Furthermore, the result would be the same – the gradual tailing off of the approach in that area. Remember the lessons of the management-by-objectives craze in the late 1960s and early 1970s. There was, and still is, nothing wrong with the concept, yet by coercing people, and by expecting everyone to change overnight, many companies alienated their managers, who responded by playing along for a while but then allowing it to die a natural death. With management by objectives, Quality Circles, or any other approach, it is not only what it is that is important, it is how it is introduced.

The second 'rule' which is often broken, usually more out of ignorance than design, is that Quality Circles are a natural workgroup approach: they comprise the supervisor and between four and ten of his workpeople. A group which contains a selection of people from different sections is a project group or task group. There is nothing wrong with project groups – it is simply that they are different. Many companies have fallen into the trap of treating project groups as if they were Quality Circles, and their programmes have suffered or even collapsed. There are a number of points to watch for here if we are to be able to learn from the experience of companies who have fallen into the trap.

Quality Circles reflect the normal management structure and therefore can work through that structure in making their proposals. This helps to reinforce two-way communication between different levels, and also minimises any threat that may be felt by managers, since they will be involved in and responsible for making decisions about any issues that affect themselves or their departments.

The objectives of a Quality Circle are to put its own house in order, and to be responsible for selecting the problems it wishes to tackle to do this. The ownership of the group by the group is the key to success. In a project group containing people from different areas and functions, there is no natural focus, no readily definable house to put in order. This usually leads to one of two outcomes. Firstly the group may find it difficult to define a problem which is of common interest without going so far up the ladder of abstraction that the problem becomes woolly, ill-defined and altogether outside the normal focus of the group. For example, groups which tackle 'the communication problem' tend to fail and become frustrated. The second outcome can be that management give problems to the group for them to tackle. This is the classic project group approach. Senior management has a particular problem, sets up an appropriate group and gives it the brief to research and report back. Again we must stress that there is nothing intrinsically wrong with this approach. Task forces are an excellent way of solving a wide range of organisational problems, but they are different from Quality Circles. If management sees its role as handing out problems to these groups, then management owns the groups and the process and the programme is in danger of becoming just another management-led, low-trust ploy. With Quality Circles it is recognised that there is expertise and experience available within the natural workgroup and that the groups are perfectly capable, given training and information, of making their own decisions about which problem to tackle.

All of this does not mean that Quality Circles have no access to other sections and departments. If they need advice, help, or information from someone else they invite the relevant people along to one or more of their meetings to help. They can also invite their manager along – indeed, this is to be encouraged – and if they wish they can ask the manager for his guidance and advice on which topics to select. The manager should feel free to put forward his views as appropriate, and should feel confident that the group will be able to make a sensible choice from the options available.

Finally on this important subject, project groups and Quality Circles are in no way mutually exclusive. Organisations practising open, participative management are likely to use both.

The other main cause of failure is inadequate resourcing. The people who will play an active role as members of Quality Circles are unlikely to have been involved in such activity before. Furthermore it should be recognised that the skills of systematic problem solving and working together in groups do not come entirely naturally. One only has to attend the average board meeting to realise this! It is essential, therefore, that Quality Circles receive sufficient training and back-up support in the early days.

There are a number of training packages specially written for Quality Circles. Some are available on the open market, while some are tied to the use of consultants. It is up to the individual companies to decide which to use or, indeed, to develop their own. It is, however, essential that good training material is used. The back-up support that groups need in the early months is provided by the facilitator, whose task it is to give help where necessary and to continue the process of training and informing and developing the Quality Circle to the point where it is self-sufficient. There is no doubt that the role is an essential one, especially in the early days, as those involved in the groups are developing their knowledge and skills. The presence of the facilitator does not, of course, preclude the manager being active in encouraging and supporting. Indeed this is an important facet of the group gaining in confidence.

Quality Circles is not an easy approach to introduce and maintain successfully. It requires skill, knowledge, commitment and perseverance. As is the case with any development of existing 'technology', there are those who say that it cannot and will not work in a Western environment. Some journalists search for their 'man bites dog' stories of failure only two years after the columns were full of the positive virtues of the approach.